Some Things to Place in a Coffin

Some Things to Place in a Coffin

Bill Manhire

Victoria University Press

TE WHARE WĀNANGA O TE ŪPOKO O TE IKA A MĀUI

VICTORIA
UNIVERSITY OF WELLINGTON

VICTORIA UNIVERSITY PRESS
Victoria University of Wellington
PO Box 600 Wellington
vup.victoria.ac.nz

Printed in China by 1010 Printing International

for Charlotte Paul

Contents

How Memory Works

Come over here
we say to the days that disappear.

No, over here.

Waiting

The window waits for light.
The path to the river waits
for twigs and stones and feet.
The day hopes to be successful,
a prose day really, nothing untoward,
and so it, too, waits. Also, the car waits.
But I suppose the car is not waiting,
it is simply taking the corners at speed –
it is the gorge that is waiting.
The family waits up all night. Sleep is useless.
We say time is of the essence, it waits
for no man. That is why China waits,
and America waits. That is why
smoke rises slowly into the air.
It is tired of waiting.

Poem in an Orchard

He was sipping tea
in the apple orchard. When I had
done with him
he was toppling forward

out of our quiet conversation
into the lower-level light,
out of family and creation
into what we have come to call the insect night

though really it is just a place of waiting,
this deep-in-the-earth despair
where the minerals complain
about their rations, and those who have gone before

also complain a little
then settle back and listen
to the helicopters settle,
terrible and terrible and not yet helpful.

Impersonating Mao

*Though she commands five-figure sums for public
appearances, Chen Yan's job has taken its toll on her marriage*

If I raise my arm to wave,
my taped breasts hurt . . . and so today
I will look at distant places: pale clouds
flaming at sunset, men on horseback,
a girl sweeping the yard. My husband
spits into the corner. Once he sang to me:
The men of the river are tired of the river.
They come ashore to sleep. And I remember
how every morning we woke in a tent.
It was always awkwardly pitched,
always in some foolish place.
Now I wake to the song of the tax collector,
and all day I stare at invisible things
until the last of the strongholds has fallen.

The Enemy

They are hiding in the reeds, in the ruins.
Almost at the gates of the city.

We have seen them before.
They knock politely. Their smile
is the grey smile of the moon.

Father says: Do not admit the one who whispers.
Mother: Nor the ones who shout and weep.
Leave them to their fate out there on the street.

You know how sometimes at night you hear a rustling
under the floorboards, some small animal . . .
or there's a burst of music over the rooftops . . .

You want to bless the world then,
you want to remember the lands
made of ice, the skies made of fire.

Soon enough the enemy will come,
limping out of a place that will not heal.

And soon enough it will be gone,
this world that you once woke into.

After the War

A man of few words
was selling words: a flower called Misery,
a tree called Roman Laughter.

He took his dictionaries from house to house.

We bought of course.

Each day the definitions shifted place.
An apple was the lift of hands to signify approval.
A rose was all that rubbish meant.

After lovemaking the young couple
opened their dictionary
to see if the world had moved.

Well, yes.

And many years later love had become
a small boat propelled by oars.

We were there in that rowboat!

I could feel it nudging the pale blank page
where only the printer's name is given.

The Question Poem

Was there a city here?

We were sitting with friends. It was a sunny day.
We were boasting about the local coffee.
Strange self-congratulations, flat whites.
These were friends we had only recently
found our way back to. For a long time
we were far apart.

Did you all survive?

On that first day of school, I mostly remember
being terrified: the dark interior, the children in rows
at their separate desks, and I was now to be one of them.
In a field by the school, there were bales of hay.
I remember inkwells.
That was perhaps a harder day.

Did you hear the bells ringing?

I keep trying to remember.
Somehow I learned to write my way round things.
The teacher made circles on the blackboard
and none of us said a word. Rubble,
then revelation: inside, we were stumbling.
And at the end of the day we all went home.

Did you all survive?

We will never sit in such places again.
A father chasing his small daughter,
both of them laughing.
The girl, a toddler, was calling out, *No, no, Matilda!*
Perhaps she knew the song from somewhere
but I think that must have been her name.

The Schoolbus

This is the place where the schoolbus turns.
The driver backs and snuffles, backs and goes.
It is always winter on these roads: high bridges
and birds in flight above you all the way.
The heart can hardly stay. The heart implodes.

The heart can hardly stay. The heart implodes.
The body gets down and walks across a field.
There are mushrooms – as in stories,
as in songs. They grow near rabbits.
Slope of hillside,

slant of rain – and here we are again:
a green-roofed house behind the trees.
The body gets down and walks across a field.
The house is full of homework fed by sleep.
A boy combs his hair, brushes his teeth,

or climbs to the top of the valley.
The sky is handkerchiefs, a single shirt.
He wants to climb higher, into a cloud.
He wants to climb into a cloud.
Whatever else is somewhere up ahead.

The schoolbus is driving through the night.
Whatever else is somewhere up ahead.
A boy keeps on hitting his head.
The small girls sing. It's nothing.
We don't know what we mean.

Is that another drink the man is pouring?
The boy turns the handle of the separator.
Cream. The boy stands on the railway line,
disappearing in rust and shine.
Goodnight Irene. Goodnight Irene.

The big door closes. A voice in the kitchen
says: Enough's enough. Running a bath.
Always cold water, boiled in pots.
The driver swears, and then he coughs.
The big door closes and you can't get off.

The Beautiful World

1.

You cannot reach the beautiful world.
It is everywhere and nowhere.
It thinks we do not know, but we do.

2.

Once I glimpsed it. My sister
opened the door and ran through.

She vanished among the trees beside the lake.
The rest of us returned to our tasks.

The place we lived was not the beautiful world.
The beautiful world is everywhere and nowhere.

You cannot reach it.

3.

I remember when I was little
my father said to my mother:

Que tu es belle!

I did not know what he meant.
I sat on the floor and watched my mother.

Then I heard him say: *Your eyes . . . tes yeux . . .*

For a moment my mother looked alarmed.

My father, too, looked alarmed . . .
he had been hoping to make her smile.

4.

A book.

It arrived in a parcel.
A man brought it on a bicycle.
He knocked at the door and blew a whistle.

I read that book a thousand times.
It knew about the beautiful world.
Each time was the very last time.

5.

House with piano. You cannot reach it.

House with stairs.
House with naughty children.

House with *The Tennessee Waltz*.

House with several fires.
House smelling of shit and toothpaste.

House with windows.
House with a garden –
flowers and vegetables – things that swim in the earth.

6.

When I grew older, I worked in a factory.
It was a cold new thing.

We made large lengths of metal
into tiny bits of metal.

The metal made an angry sound
each time you looked at it.

But you had to look at it.

7.

It was not her lovely eyes.
I think it was her lovely hair.

It was not the trees.
It was somewhere beyond the trees.
It was not the window or the lake.
It was the lake seen from the window,

there for a moment each morning.

8.

There was a park in that city
where we all assembled.
One edge was the edge of the woods.

A man ran out of the woods, shouting,
and into the city, shouting.

Then the gunfire and the rain began.

9.

The beautiful world is sad . . .
so all the travellers say.

People there grow vegetables,
They smoke *cheroots*
and keep a goat.

Otherwise they do nothing.
All day they dream about their dreams.

10.

So much cold came out of the earth,
we could not talk about it.

Was there some way to make it stop?

Branches laid on the earth,
bits of metal, planks, old blankets.

But the cold kept on rising.
We shivered and could not talk about it.

It was in the wings of angels
in the graveyard where we walked.

It rose around my sister's empty bed.

It rose around my father, who seemed lost.

It rose around my mother, who was gone.

11.

Two men kicked down the door.
They shouted, then they stood still.

This is interesting, said the shorter one.

I was alone in the house.
The other man said nothing.
He walked quickly away.

12.

It does not want to be beautiful.
It wants to live in a house.

But it cannot live in a house.

It wants a family.

But it needs too many rooms.

13.

Then where are the birds going?
Where is the helicopter going?
Where is the sky going, with all its clouds?

Over here! we call. *Over here!*

14.

~~Where our sister has opened the door.~~

~~Where our father stands beside our mother.~~

Where the trees have gathered to admire the water.

Surveillance Notes

In Sweden, they whispered all winter,
counting the frozen minutes.
In France, they branched out. Tips of experience.
In England, they dreamed of Ireland.
In Ireland they seemed to be lonely.
Germany was Belgium then was Spain.
Italy was something else again.
Portugal, Portugal, Portugal:
they said that a lot because they never went back.
Later in Hungary, he lay on his back
and watched the clouds – so few of them
but each one big and fluffy. In the first dream,
the angel was having a dream; in the next dream
the angel still clung to his story.

Coastal Farewell

Just behind the caravan
where the worried man sold coffee,
that's where they fell in love.

Then, well, you know how it goes – the girl
wants to journey east, then further east;
the man, still worried, says he might stay put.

Thus a few weeks later they stand together
for perhaps the last time. One speaks,
the other doesn't . . .

It's true, this is like some ancient Chinese poem
from the something-or-other Dynasty.
The weather hums. It has a missing tooth.

Learning

Here is the other language,
all zigzags and bad decisions,
the light that shines but can't remember,
the pond with its elegant elbows,
the toddler yelling at a single duck.

Ten minutes later, everything is different.
A trail down to the water.
Cold riddle, cold lament.
For a moment the raft
is reachable, then it isn't.

Homeric

Cold cry from the last page of the dictionary,
name with a knife in it, and the knife
italic against the throat

till you fall into so heavy a sleep –
sleep made of asterisks and cattle,
the herd just a black scarf

against snow – you can't begin to guess
where the old world went. Now there are only two
choices, says the tale, and neither is good.

Hence an axe above each separate entrance
as the hero becomes hardly a voice
and the sad dogs appear on the screen.

Then there is a thin, high scraping.
Then no noise of any sort at all.

My World War I Poem

Inside each trench, the sound of prayer.
Inside each prayer, the sound of digging.

Known unto God

To you, your name also,
Did you think there was nothing but two or three
*   pronunciations in the sound of your name?*

—Walt Whitman

Boy on horseback,
boy on a bicycle, boy all the way
from Tolaga Bay

blown to bits in a minute.

Once I was small bones
in my mother's body
just taking a nap.
Now my feet can't find the sap.

In Devil's Wood
I broke my leg and went beneath a tank.
Strange beast! Last thing I heard
was the guns all going, you know,
blankety-blankety-blank.

My last letter home
turned out entirely pointless.
I wrote *whizz-bang*
a dozen times

to try and say the noises.

Well I was here from the start, amazing . . .
straight off the farm at Taieri Mouth.

I lifted my head and ran like the blazes.
Went south.

I whistled while I could.
Then I was gone for good.

So strange to be underground and single
and dreaming of Dunedin.

But such a picnic!

The last thing I saw
was a tin of Ideal Milk.

I remember my father and my mother.
They yelled, they cursed.

My whole head hurt.

Up on the wire I couldn't hear a thing.
I who had spent my whole life listening.

They dug me up in Caterpillar Valley
and brought me home –
well, all of the visible bits of me.

Now people arrive at dawn and sing.
And I have a new word: *skateboarding*.

Not all of me is here inside.
I built Turk Lane before I died.

Kia ahatia!

Somewhere between Colombo and Cairo,
the ocean seemed to dip. I thought I could hear
the stamping of horses coming from it.

They taught me how to say *refugee*.
Then my father and mother floated away from me.

This was on the way to Lampedusa.
By now we were all at sea.

We were all at sea.

They called out while they could.

~~They called out while they could~~.

Then they were gone for good.

Rescue

I was talking to the man who suffers
and I was talking to the man who sings
boys still jumping off the railway bridge
like small boys in a dream

and there's always time for something special
and there's always time for time like now
and there's always time for making up our differences
we get along so well

I was talking to the man who dredged the river
and I was talking to the driver of the train
he tried to take his engine sideways
like an engine driver in a dream

and there's always time for going to the party
and there's always someone going wow
and there's always time for going crazy
we get along so well

I was walking past the big white hospital
it isn't really white, it's cream
the lines of cars keep getting longer
each one of them delivering . . .

and there's always time to say you're sorry
always one last chance to break the spell
and there's always a loving friend who pulls you sideways
we get along so well

My First Hit

I woke up in another lover's song.

It said: are you a good person or a bad person?
and where you were during the instrumental?
I can't decide I can't decide

Guess I'll wait around in the chorus
it's the one place where I miss you
one place where I miss you

Now love yes it makes me guess at the world
Love makes my tears to fall
from this other song I'm listening to

It's true, it's true, it's true

don't like the elephant
don't like the monkey
don't like the king
don't like the flunky

rpt

They've all walked in from another song
from another lover's song.
A melody like that you can't go wrong
it's sad to wake up in another lover's song

Gold Goes Platinum

The necessary thing, where did it go.
oh oh oh oh
each night the moonlight's saying no
no no no no

I was trying to read Stalky & Co
I was trying to read Stalky & Co
oh oh oh oh oh oh oh

I lost my place I was losing face
I don't like Rudyard Kipling
but man that man can sing.

Rikkitikkitavi
you're so charming
Rikkitikkitavi
oh my darling

Rikkitikkitavi
you're so charming
Rikkitikkitavi
oh my darling

I can't believe your tender kiss
I can't believe your tenderness
The end of empire is a special emptiness
The end of empire is a special emptiness

My Sad Girls

My sad girls are singing –
some sort of song, some sort of where
have the words gone wrong, oh I am
a widowed man without a song.

Soon I will leave this place
and go to find the mother. In the wide world
only she will know
why you are out so late my girls,

why each with only the other
for companion, daughter and daughter and just
the memory of a mother, and over your heads
the cold words go.

I hear you calling now across the worlds
to tell how you are destitute.
Her name, says the song, is Raukatauri.
She lives inside her flute.

Poem Beginning with a Line by Yeats

I made it out of a mouthful of air.
Foolish balloon that bounced

from hand to hand
like a difficult

friend at a party. But you
weren't even

there, says the difficult
friend in question.

Get out of here!

You mouthful of cheese.
You morsel.

Sunday School Mural

The hill looks like a long-haired, bearded man
and Primrose and Jessica are climbing it.
Their arms wave. They jump and sing.
There are stabs in their heads where the crosses go.

Much of the human race is made of gravel, some bits
are scrub and tussock, then high up snow.
The summit is the top, where you can see the sea.
People put flags there. Jess says to Primrose: Follow me.

And so the girls go clambering.
The day is pleasant. Nothing much
is going on that hasn't. Yes we have heard
of God and the devil, of things going round,

we have all the details. One has a hammer,
the other has nails – look there's a cross!
We jump and we sing, and we feel our way forward
when most we are lost.

Christmas

Evening: the nervous suburbs levitate.
Height does us no harm, now we are high above the mineral pools,
above the flash hotel whose only use is treachery.
Someone knocks on a door and you crouch behind the bed.

Down in the bar, the small girls toast their parents,
the brother breaks a large bone for its marrow.
I'm thinking of a challenge for us all. The star in the sky
has travelled all the way from home. Now follow that!

20 Stanzas in the Haunted House

So the ghost appeared
and asked could he recite one of his poems.
OK, I said, feeling a little strange, just a little bit
frightened. Of course I don't actually believe in ghosts
but this one seemed legitimate and spooky. The poem
itself was a quite long poem, all about wind and water
and navigating by the stars, and he declaimed it
in an uncannily spectral manner,
so that when his words finally reached shore
I was just about asleep. I could hear lake-water lapping.
What do you think? he said. I would really
welcome your comments. To be honest, I replied,
I can't imagine any way you could begin to make that poem better.
I really liked the 22nd stanza. He turned then and cursed me,
cursed the *Paris Review*, cursed all my issue,
and slowly dissolved in the mirror.

Election Address

I expect you know why I have asked you here
at this late hour. The stars, gentlemen, the stars!
They shine as ever, here at *End-of-the-line*.
Do sit awhile and admire the heavens.
I have robes and a chain, and I have power
in useful ways: your electricity
is mine, as is the public swimming pool.
I license the posts you hope to score beneath.
I can require the trams to go more slowly, for as you know
at speed they wildly sway from side to side.
Indeed I pledge now to slow them. Also I retain
the men who plant flower after flower
along our rugged coast. And yet it is true
End-of-the-line suffers from its libraries,
by which I do not mean a money thing.
No. People should not be handling our books
when they spit and dress like that. And ocean gales
come constantly to harry us,
and seaweed and driftwood, which we gather,
can barely compensate. Oh we live in an old something
of the sun, and yes, I get many letters, rates,
I read them all. Drains or pigeons? Make a wish!
I do not care, sir, that you do not swim.
Yes, I was troubled by the recent earthquake.
I do not believe that I am rubbish.

My Early Life

My father was a mountain-climber who finished life as a school
    janitor.
I never knew his real name, everyone called him Burp.
He always encouraged me though.
The household had little money but there was always food on the
    table.
Sometimes my mother would disappear mysteriously for days.
Burp was never troubled. Maybe he knew where she went all along.
Our neighbours on one side had a turbulent marriage but even so we
    were a small but close-knit community.
At quite a young age there were glimpses of my future talent . . .
People all commented how talented I was.
Also, I was resourceful. Everyone said.
I had a newspaper round to help pay for my lessons.
Mostly I delivered magazines all the way from London.
However being the last of six surviving children, I never felt truly
    loved.
I felt I had been stolen from my real parents.
Such things fuelled my early vision.
I once fell down a steep ravine and was subsequently found by search
    dogs.
For a time after that I suffered from memory loss.
I remember the doctor saying, 'This kid is full of gaps. Let's party
    like there's no tomorrow.'
This was before things really took off.
Later we moved from rented room to rented room.
All our possessions could fit in the palm of your hand.
Lucky for me, my hand got bigger.
My first competitive success was no surprise, at least to me.

I made my first feature film while still in high school.
I lived in a caravan with some hired caregivers.
They had travelled all the way from New Zealand.
Every morning they did drugs and set out the muesli.
They taught me how to pray and apply make-up in a fully
    professional manner.
The first time I picked up a guitar, everyone around applauded.
One chord after another: that was the secret.
In those days, each friend was a good friend.
I would watch the gangsters, pimps, and wrestlers wander through
    the night.
I was criticised for my stiff manner, my squint, and for hissing the
    words through my teeth.
Little did people know I had a secret life as a satirist.
I called myself *The Flim and the Flam*.
I knew that one day I would break some big stories in the cultural
    space.
One weekend I asked Burp what his real name was, and he said,
'Ask your mother.' But my mother hadn't been home for weeks.
And in fact I was now embarked on my subsequent career
and I never did see her again.

Mrs Zeus

In her dream she lived in a high apartment
with a few small children. She looked down at the rain.
Gulls fought over bread, over the alphabet.
Her new husband walked to work every day.
Lucky man – he hated driving.
She had only married him to change her name.
Mrs Acorn! She would always be first in the queue.

What Will Last

It is hard to know what will last. I don't think the things we think will last will last, do you? You never know what will matter. When I left school-teaching I was presented with a miniature tank, a fighting machine I had never personally been involved with during all my years in the territorials. I kept it, the tank, in appearance it was very detailed, on my mantelpiece for many years, but I now seem to have lost it. But something else is there in its place, I know this for a fact, though just at the moment I cannot remember what it is. I think I still love music. I am in the wrong room in the house at the moment, that is the heart of the problem, and I am not sure that I can find my way back. But I do think that that particular thing, whatever it is, will last, don't you.

*

The music in my heart I bore long after it was heard no more.

Now who said that?

*

Madame Duvet. She was all feathers. Her eyelashes were so long they cast a shadow across the crowded auditorium. I attended her establishment for many months before gaining admission to her chamber. What more can I say? One glorious night. She left me a single feather, and I have it still.

*

I know a man who knew a man who knew a man who owns a pair of Rupert Brooke's underpants. The man is what they call a fellow at what they call a college at a place known to all and sundry as the University of Cambridge. He will be a scholar or something, but a scholar of what, well I don't know. How do you find out these things? Anyway, he has this most unusual possession. The man who told me about him says he keeps the underpants in a transparent box in a special drawer in what are called his rooms, or is it his chambers. Or maybe kept is a better word. He is probably dead now, the underpants man as I call him.

*

All the same, God has made some terrific tourist locations. I managed to get the rights to one some years ago. A cataract, a canyon. That was just the start of it. I lost the contract three years later in an international bidding war. When I kneel in prayer, I remember it all clearly. So in a sense, and in a somewhat spiritual way, I have it still. Photographs, the paint charts etc. You do not even need to believe in God. You kneel in the middle of the airport concourse, just a bit of a rest for a moment, then people come and help you to your feet. Now you have a memory that will last forever.

*

Probably ancient coins will last. I have a biscuit-tin full of sixpences and threepenny bits. They rattle around in there, though actually they are too heavy to rattle. Likewise the sound of people waiting quietly in the next-door room. I think that will last.

*

Also, things that rhyme! I think the past will last, even when we all forget it.

*

Wordsworth!

The Poet

Harmonious lovely girl is writing me a letter.
Her shirt falls open
at the dark desk where she sits.
Oh she takes a thousand different forms,
that is the truth of it. Maybe she is wearing jodhpurs
or is nearly naked, tuning her lute.
Go from the window, my dear,
you cannot be lodged here . . .
Her voice when she begins to sing
is always mildly troubling.

I check out her busy November schedule
and note that I am nowhere in it.
She is like an ocean made of plastic bags.
No one can swim there
though sometimes the truly brazen float.
You hear applause each time they hit another boat.
The rest of us sit and watch the barrage.
We are mostly missing persons.
We hate October.
We hate October and all its sinkings.

Well I will ride out through the furious woods
where nothing is harmonious.
My life has become almost a scream
from all the galloping. There is nothing
new under the sun, yet this is where
my best ideas come from. Yes, most of us

are mostly harmless: we all have tote bags
which we tote. Meanwhile the high trees rest,
the children sleep, the wind gets up.
A horse is more than its harness.

Indexing Emily

The dead gaze back across their special days:
cloud above clover, crisis above the crow . . .
Such new horizons, yet they still approach.
They know how eclipse and ecstacy edge along together:
whisper and wink of wind, but no real weather.

Between practice and prayer there's always praise.
Mist and mistakes are in the text.
And now here's the night – nobody's next – and poetry
falls from the crucifixion like a crumb, and belief
needs bells, needs bereavement. Bothersome.

Now a feather falls towards March
somehow recalling the snake above the snow.
Everything slows. All those ships
anticipating shipwreck: frigate, little boat.
Brain almost touching the bride. Sweet anecdote.

Can the simple be simplified? Our riches
ride on a riddle: rapture and rainbow
and remaining time. And now all the columns
of Love appear. No word of reproof, no sign
of rage. Love is like Death: it needs to turn the page.

The Philosopher's Children

The philosopher's children
play in their own special room.

They pinch themselves.
They cry, Aha!

'Nothing comes from nothing,'
they say, quoting someone or something.

Parmenides possibly
or maybe *The Sound of Music.*

We are not allowed to play with them.
Instead we must endure our mother's tears,
our uncle's deep-throated chant.

'Is this red ball a ball
in quite the way

that this blue ball
might be said to be a ball?'

That's what my sister says to me
whenever the philosopher's children
hide behind the fence to listen.

But the ball she is holding
is grey and pointless.

Then she laughs and pinches me, and runs away.

Fahrenheit

That was the autumn my father died. His dying involved long and then longer visits to the hospice, plus the unlikely presence of my brother and sister. They had flown in from their particular foreign cities but chose to stay in a local hotel, taking turns to complain about the heat. Weirdly, what I remember most from that time is the morning I noticed the new neighbour staring over the fence. It was early in the day, and he stood there a long time. He seemed to be looking towards my house but also far into the distance. When I went over, he introduced himself as Dr Fahrenheit, and told me, by way of explaining his gaze, that he was hoping to catch sight of his wife, who had, as he put it, 'wandered off'. It was a strange encounter, and we never progressed beyond those first, awkward civilities. If the wife existed, I never saw her. Now a young family lives next door. Sometimes a ball will appear on the lawn and a small boy comes round to fetch it. As for Dr Fahrenheit, over the years since our brief exchange I have formulated several clumsy jokes, all to do with temperature, and have always felt pleased that I did not make them.

Some Things to Place in a Coffin

Hardboard and canvas, some leadhead nails.
A blowtorch, a spray-gun, a grinder.
A glass of pinot noir.
A boat with a motor, a boat with sails, a boat with oars.
France and Spain.
Some Lorca, some lacquer.
A fishing rod, a hammer.
The dog Matiu.
Timber & bricks. A Tiger Moth.
Some rope, some sky, some ocean.
The Stations of the Cross.
A coil of number 8 wire.
A slowness. A suddenness. A concentrating grunt.
Vidyapati's Song.
Smoke & flags & banners.
The far north. The deep south.
Harbour Cone.
A home-made home.
The bishop, the knight, the rook.
A black Union Jack.
A circle, a line, a cross.
Some words & numbers.
Some corrugations.
Nailed down with iron against the rain.
Nailed down with rain.
With daisies.
With weather.
With gold.
With an old window-frame.

Falseweed

Poor tanglebell, trying
so hard to ring
and barely coughing

*

& leafcandle flickering –

*

each recalling
his long-lost cousin

wintertwig

feeling my way
       feeling my way

but already lost
in the twilight.

Now darkness brings out
the little paperclip

plus a clump or two
of scribblegrass –

*

If we had seeds
we would scatter them

scatter them –

*

oh pencilheart –
oh smudge-of-lead.

That said . . .

I saw how breeze in the chaingrass
made the small chains sing,

I began to recall
how the words came knocking.

ribslip, waterpath, absentee

When I was a child I thought as a child.

I walked each day in a ditch
made of bones & bumblebees.

*

A field away, sheep shat.

*

Cows carried their milk
across the cream-and-cheese.

Wintertwig back again?

                                    yes

yet all at sea —

lonely too

missing the old company —

lost-kiss

          anchorweed

                    tongue-true

The water itself long gone

*

like the departing day

*

like all our talk

*

but look
where the *arawai*

holds on

*

stuttering on its stalk.

& anchorwhite –

always going
always gone again.

*

The heavy trees
do not want him –

they shower him with bark & leaf
with can't-complain

*

now he is all duress
attached to *whim* –

he falls apart,
they smother him.

But how sad to be sad!

Consider the thornwing:

*

how it hums & hahs

& hums & hahs

all through the night . . .

*

then pricks the air

*

in order

to take flight

The Lake

The lake is happy when the sky clouds over.
It has nothing left to give.

The girl sings the songs that she is given,
songs that are held at the threshold.

Her gift is expected, or unexpected.
There is no other gift.

I closed my invisible book.
I tried to stand.

Rapture. Quiet canoe.
I was defeated, done with speaking.

Acknowledgements

Australian Book Review, Cordite, Cyphers, Eggbox Publishing, Ika, London Review of Books, PN Review, Poetry, Poetry Ireland, Poetry London, The Spinoff, Sport, Turbine.

'Known unto God' was part of the *Fierce Light* co-commission by 14–18 NOW, Norfolk & Norwich Festival and Writers' Centre Norwich, commemorating the Battle of the Somme.

'Rescue' is a song lyric written for the musician SJD.

'Some Things to Place in a Coffin' was written in memory of Ralph Hotere, whose coffin was heavier than it should have been.

DOUBT, FAITH, AND CERTAINTY

DOUBT, FAITH, AND CERTAINTY

Anthony C. Thiselton

WILLIAM B. EERDMANS PUBLISHING COMPANY
GRAND RAPIDS, MICHIGAN

Wm. B. Eerdmans Publishing Co.
2140 Oak Industrial Drive NE, Grand Rapids, Michigan 49505
www.eerdmans.com

Published 2017
Printed in the United States of America

23 22 21 20 19 18 17   1 2 3 4 5 6 7

ISBN 978-0-8028-7353-8

Library of Congress Cataloging-in-Publication Data

Names: Thiselton, Anthony C., author.
Title: Doubt, faith, and certainty / Anthony C. Thiselton.
Description: Grand Rapids, Michigan : William B. Eerdmans Publishing Company, [2017] |
    Includes bibliographical references and index.
Identifiers: LCCN 2016047030 | ISBN 9780802873538 (paperback : alk. paper)
Subjects: LCSH: Faith.
Classification: LCC BT771.3 .T46 2017 | DDC 234/.23—dc23
    LC record available at https://lccn.loc.gov/2016047030

Contents

Abbreviations

ANF	*Ante-Nicene Fathers*
BDAG	W. Bauer, F. W. Danker, W. F. Arndt, and F. W. Gingrich, *A Greek-English Lexicon of the New Testament and Other Early Christian Literature* (3rd ed.; Chicago: University of Chicago Press, 2000)
KJV	King James Version
NIV	New International Version
NJB	New Jerusalem Bible
NPNF¹	*Nicene and Post-Nicene Fathers*, series 1
NRSV	New Revised Standard Version

Preface

This book carries a simple message. On *doubt*, it argues that while some
degree of doubt in some circumstances may perhaps be bad, in different
situations doubts may stimulate us to fresh thought and questioning. In fact
the message remains the same for *doubt*, *faith*, and *certainty*: none of these
terms has a uniform meaning, or has a uniform function in life. They have
a *variety* of meanings.

I originally hoped to write for all kinds of readers, since the pres-
ence or absence of doubt, faith, and certainty causes endless anxiety and
heart-searching for all kinds of people. Those who might be undergoing
depression of trauma often doubt a constant threat and challenge, and I seek
to show that doubt may sometimes have a positive role. I have been greatly
helped in this respect by Rev. Stuart Dyas, who has regularly pushed me to be
more explanatory, more specific, and less reliant on technical philosophical
terms, in order to reach a wider, nonspecialist, readership. This subject, how-
ever, raises unavoidable philosophical questions, and at times a simplified
and explanatory philosophical discussion had to be included.

I have endeavored to discuss such philosophical questions in as basic a
way as possible. It is unavoidable, however, to discuss, for example, the early
skeptics Descartes and Locke and especially the approaches of Wittgenstein
and Plantinga. I postponed treatment of both of these difficult and complex
thinkers, but also highly suggestive and productive ones, until chapter 7,
which is probably the most technical philosophical discussion. Those who

know my work will not be surprised that I have found Pannenberg especially fruitful on eschatological certainty.

I was intrigued to consider the relation between supposed certainty and probability in different contexts in life. These contexts include legal certainty, certainty in statistics, and most of all certainty in physics and other sciences. John Polkinghorne and many others show how different the situation has become since Heisenberg, Dirac, and others. Many are reluctant to speak of anything beyond a high degree of probability.

The important thing, however, is that those who entertain doubts should not assume that all doubt is bad or condemned by God. Doubt and questioning may open the door to new insights and to a needed reappraisal of faith or belief. Similarly, many Christians, as well as others, assume that faith always denotes *one* thing, when it can mean *many* possible things. Finally, many assumptions about supposed certainty fail to attend to very different contexts in which certainty may be claimed. Some who claim for themselves absence of doubt and possession of utter certainty may possibly be masking a degree of arrogance behind a display of piety.

The biblical writings and the Holy Spirit anticipate partial certainty, which is yet to be vindicated in the future. Paul reminds us: "Now I know only in part; then I will know fully" (1 Cor. 13:12). Meanwhile faith features for the Christian alongside hope and love. But doubt, faith, and certainty must always be examined from one situation to another. Each has many different meanings, according to their situation.

I should like to give warm thanks to those who have helped me to produce this book. My wife, Rosemary, has done much of the typing. I am especially grateful to Sheila Rees for meticulous proofreading of the entire manuscript. Conversations with Dr. Tim Hull were helpful. Once again, however, I must acknowledge special thanks to Stuart Dyas, not only for careful proofreading of the typescript, but also for numerous stylistic improvements, which will help nonspecialist readers.

CHAPTER 1

The Various Meanings of Doubt, Faith, and Certainty

The Various Meanings of Doubt

The different meanings and significances of doubt constitute an immensely practical and potentially liberating pastoral and intellectual issue. It is a practical disaster that in popular thought some view all doubt as a sign of weakness and lack of faith; while others, by contrast, extol doubt as always a sign of mature, sophisticated reflection.

In popular Christian thought many regard doubt simply as lack of faith or lack of trust in God. Those who admit to having doubts are often accused of confusion, irresolution, hesitancy, skepticism, reluctance to take a stand, or endless postponement of bold commitment. Even worse, some regard doubters as disobedient, distrustful, faithless, vacillating, and wavering.

John Suk produced a remarkable and moving book entitled *Not Sure: A Pastor's Journey from Faith to Doubt*. He explains: "Doubt has turned me back to theology and Scripture with attention to detail that I haven't known since studying for seminary exams. Doubt reveals texts I used to skip over because they were obtuse, difficult, or didn't easily fit the picture I expected to see. . . . Doubt is like a new set of glasses: you see more."[1] But he also considers the other side of the coin. He writes that doubt "also hurts. . . . Doubt has also put enormous stress on my marriage. . . . How

---

1. John Suk, *Not Sure: A Pastor's Journey from Faith to Doubt* (Grand Rapids: Eerdmans, 2011), 4.

difficult it is to reconsider [comfortable faith] . . . for something new and uncertain."[2]

Examples occur in the Bible of both interpretations of doubt, in different circumstances. Jesus certainly laments a divided self. When Peter walked to him over the waves but began to sink when he doubted, Jesus said to him: "You of little faith, why did you doubt [*ti edistasas*]?" (Matt. 14:31 NIV). The same word is used latter in Matthew: "They worshiped him; but some doubted" (28:17 NIV). The Greek *distazō* means "to waver, have two minds, be double-minded." James warns us against double-mindedness, using the Greek word *diakrino-menos* ("one who doubts") in 1:6 and *dipsychos* ("double-minded") in 4:8. Luke uses *dialogismos* ("doubting") in Luke 24:38. Luke and Paul use *aporeō* (Luke 24:4; Gal. 4:20) to denote "perplexity, confusion, or being at a loss."[3]

On the other side, popular thought often neglects the entirely positive meanings of the term "doubt." A person who never admits any doubt about anything may rightly be regarded as heartless, insensitive, overconfident, or arrogant. Doubt about one's convictions constitutes the beginning of self-criticism, correction, discovery, and more mature insight. We need not subscribe to his entire philosophy to see the point of Sir William Hamilton's telling aphorism: "We doubt in order that we may believe."[4] Where belief is exposed to be mere opinion or prejudice, doubt may provide a path to authentic belief. In politics an overconfident government may rush headlong with premature decisions without due reflection.

In philosophy Socrates remains the classic case for encouraging doubt as the first step toward knowledge, or toward distinguishing authentic belief from mere opinion. Some regard the doubts of Thomas the apostle as leading toward a more firmly founded faith. In modern times Gregory Boyd attacks the avoidance of all doubt concerning the Christian faith, especially in a Pentecostal context: "This *certainty-seeking* concept of faith is causing a great deal of *harm* to the church today."[5] He explains: "I once assumed a person's

---

2. Ibid., 4–5.

3. BDAG 119, 232–34, 252; and J. H. Thayer, *Greek-English Lexicon of the New Testament*, 4th ed. (Edinburgh: T&T Clark, 1901), 66, 141, 152–53.

4. William Hamilton, *The Metaphysics of Sir William Hamilton* (London: Forgotten Books, 2013 [orig. 1863]), 57.

5. Gregory A. Boyd, *Benefit of Doubt: Breaking the Idol of Certainty* (Grand Rapids: Baker, 2013), 13 (emphasis added).

faith is as strong as that person is certain. And, accordingly, I assumed that doubt is the enemy of faith. That is . . . how Christians generally talk."[6]

Admittedly in the biblical writings the actual word "doubt" occurs more frequently with negative implications than positive ones. Nevertheless much of the Bible enjoins humility and the limits of knowledge. Moreover the Bible often provides examples of the need for critical reflection. The Old Testament uses *ḥîdâ* ("to test with hard questions"; 1 Kings 10:1; 2 Chron. 9:1), *dāraš* ("to question"; 2 Chron. 31:9), or *'āmar lô* ("to think or to say to oneself "; Esth. 6:6). Like the Hebrew *ḥāšab* ("to reckon"; Ps. 119:59), all four of these Hebrew terms suggest a period of careful and critical thought before plunging into premature conclusions.[7] The Piel form of the verb *ḥāšab* suggests a human capacity to view issues self-critically.[8]

The New Testament also commends "thinking" in the sense of reflecting critically on options. Jesus asks Peter: "What do you think [*dokeō*], Simon?" (Matt. 17:25 NIV). The verb *dokeō* forbids glib or premature answers. Thus after a parable, Jesus asks: "What do you think?" (18:12 NIV). The verb *dokeō* occurs sixty-two times in the New Testament. In Classical Greek it initiates the reflection that distinguishes reality or truth from mere opinion or appearance (e.g., Parmenides 28B.8.50–51, and frequently in Plato).

Ian Ramsey argues that some degree of doubt can deliver us from seeming to be "certain" about every possible aspect of religion. He argues: "The desire to be sure in religion leads, it will be said, to *prejudice, bigotry, and fanaticism*."[9] An orthodox Christian believer who is not skeptical about the core values of Christian faith, Ramsey also insists that if we think that *anything at all* remains beyond doubt, this might constitute symptoms of arrogance or bumptiousness. He cites Joseph Butler (1692–1752) and F. D. Maurice (1805–72) as admitting to certain doubts about such doctrines as universal final destiny.

Doubt, then, can function either negatively as a term that stands in contrast to trust, faith, or wholeheartedness; or positively as a term to denote self-criticism, humility, and careful reflection. Often only attention to the

---

6. Ibid., 13.

7. K. Seybold, "*Chāshab*," in *Theological Dictionary of the Old Testament*, ed. G. J. Botterweck and Helmut Ringgren (Grand Rapids: Eerdmans, 1986), 5.228–45.

8. Ibid., 5.245.

9. Ian T. Ramsey, *On Being Sure in Religion* (London: Athlone, 1963), 2 (emphasis added).

context of the word "doubt" will indicate the sense in which it is to be under-
stood. I note this in connection with faith and certainty as well. Philosophers
and those who specialize in linguistics often use the term "polymorphous"
to denote those words that vary their meaning in accordance with their
context. This linguistic phenomenon is more widespread than we might at
first imagine.

Linguistic philosophers Friedrich Waismann and Ludwig Wittgenstein
provide an abundance of illustrations from everyday language. Waismann
selects the word "to try" as a significant example that we can all readily un-
derstand. On a sleepless night we may "try" to get to sleep. But the meaning
of "try" here is quite different from when we "try" to lift a heavy weight, or
"try" to play the piano better, or "try" to free ourselves from bonds. "To try,"
he observes, "is used in many different and differently related ways."[10]

Wittgenstein also provides a number of examples. Perhaps "playing a
game" constitutes the most well known. What playing consists in depends
on whether the context is that of card games, board games, athletics, quizzes,
and so on. In contrast to expounding the genuinely polymorphous nature
of many words, Wittgenstein rightly comments on the root cause of their
neglect: "Our craving for generality . . . our pre-occupation with the method
of science . . . leads the philosopher into complete darkness. . . . Instead of
'craving for generality,' I could also have said 'the contemptuous attitude
towards the particular case.'"[11] Some concepts are *partly* polymorphous.
Wittgenstein calls these "concepts with blurred edges."[12]

Philosophical linguist William Alston makes a similar point about the
vagueness of many words. He selects the everyday example of being mid-
dle aged, to which I refer later. Alston explains: "A term is said to be *vague*
if there are cases in which there is no definite answer as to whether the
term applies."[13] Thus some people seem middle aged before they reach forty,
while many argue that 45–65 seems to offer a more respectable definition.

10. Friedrich Waismann, *The Principles of Linguistic Philosophy* (London: Macmillan,
1965), 183–84.

11. Ludwig Wittgenstein, *The Blue and Brown Books: Preliminary Studies for the "Philo-
sophical Investigations,"* 2nd ed. (Oxford: Blackwell, 1969), 18.

12. Ludwig Wittgenstein, *Philosophical Investigations,* 2nd ed. (Oxford: Blackwell, 1958),
§§71–72.

13. William P. Alston, *Philosophy of Language* (Englewood Cliffs, NJ: Prentice-Hall, 1964),
84.

We cannot legislate for a universal definition. Alston concludes: "We need vague terms for situations like this," that is, in politics, demography, and diplomacy.[14]

Paul Tillich provides one example in which doubt would have a necessary place. He insists on the need to search for God beyond the "god" of an inadequate or distorted concept, picture, or understanding. He comments that some may imagine that they are rejecting God when "it is not he whom we reject and forget, but . . . rather some distorted picture of him."[15] At a popular level this could be a God of mistaken or inadequate elementary Sunday School instruction. At a more sophisticated level, Tillich declares: "The god whom we can easily bear, a god from whom we do not have to hide, a god whom we do not hate in moments . . . is not God at all."[16] Dietrich Bonhoeffer voices broadly similar concerns. Doubt may sometimes lead to a revised concept of God. He writes: "I either know about the God I seek from my own experience. . . . Or I know about him based on his revelation of his own Word. Either I determine the place in which I will find God, or I allow God to determine the place where he will be found."[17] Bonhoeffer explains further that to find "the God who in some way corresponds to me . . . fits in with my nature" is a false path: "God is not agreeable to me at all . . . does not fit so well with me. That place is the place of the cross."[18] Doubt, again, may be the beginning of self-criticism and may set us on the path toward a more authentic view of God.

In this book I aim to demonstrate the various meanings not only of doubt, but also of faith and certainty. I argue elsewhere that this principle applies to biblical uses of "flesh" (Greek *sarx*) and in certain respects to "truth."[19] In very crude terms doubt can be "bad" or "good" according to its context. We must next explore some introductory considerations about the various meanings of faith and certainty.

---

14. Ibid., 86.

15. Paul Tillich, *The Shaking of the Foundations* (New York: Scribner, 1948), 49.

16. Ibid., 50.

17. Dietrich Bonhoeffer, *Meditating on the Word* (Cambridge, MA; Cowley, 1986), 44.

18. Ibid., 45.

19. Anthony C. Thiselton, *The Two Horizons* (Grand Rapids: Eerdmans/Exeter: Paternoster, 1980), 408–15.

The Various Meanings of Faith

The New Testament writings do not uniformly present a single meaning of faith. Rudolf Bultmann argues that in Paul it denotes trust, reliance, and confidence. But he recognizes that in Paul faith (Greek *pistis*) also means "the acceptance of the kerygma" or "gospel message."[20] It is not, he insists, a psychological state. Especially in Galatians and Romans it can "only be committed to God's grace . . . the opposite of every work or achievement."[21] He sees Christian faith in contrast to Judaism as letting the self go in trust in God. Bultmann writes in his *Theology of the New Testament* exactly what he said in *Theological Dictionary of the New Testament*. But he also complicates matters by claiming in his *Theology*: "*Paul understands faith primarily as obedience*, as if this did not depend on Paul's context of argument.[22] It is sometimes "acceptance of the message," at other times "primarily . . . obedience" (Rom. 16:19); and at yet others, reliance upon God or trust. Bultmann adds in the context of justification by grace: "Faith's attitude is the radical opposite of the attitude of 'boasting.'"[23] Thus it is "the radical renunciation of accomplishment."[24] In addition to the three or four meanings already offered, Bultmann declares that "it is *simultaneously confession*." Furthermore, he rightly notes, "Faith always has reference to its object," that is, it relates closely to God or Jesus Christ, which is decisive for its meaning.[25]

Typically, in view of his Lutheran tradition, Bultmann cites paradigmatic examples of faith. In Galatians 2:16 Paul declares: "A person is justified not by the works of the law but through faith in Jesus Christ" (NRSV). In 2:20 he states: "The life I now live . . . I live by faith in the Son of God" (NRSV). Romans 3:22 speaks of "the righteousness of God through faith in Jesus Christ"; and 3:26 declares that God justifies "the one who has faith in Christ." Philippians 3:9 echoes the contrast between observance of the law and "what comes to us through faith in Christ." Faith is regularly "faith in" (Greek *pis-*

---

20. Rudolf Bultmann, "*Pisteuō, Pistis*," in *Theological Dictionary of the New Testament*, ed. G. Kittel (Grand Rapids: Eerdmans, 1968), 6.174–228 at 217.

21. Ibid., 6.219–20.

22. Rudolf Bultmann, *Theology of the New Testament* (London: SCM, 1952), 1.314–15 (emphasis original).

23. Ibid., 1.315.

24. Ibid., 1.316.

25. Ibid., 1.317 (emphasis original).

teuō eis) or "faith that" (*pisteuō hoti*). The noun "faith" usually translates the Greek noun *pistis*, while the verbal form "I believe" usually translates *pisteuō*. For example: "We believe that if we have died with him, we shall also live with him" (Rom. 6:8).

The meanings that Bultmann attributes to "faith" in Paul alone are so various that we might be tempted to imagine that Bultmann exaggerated or became confused. However, within the last five years Jonathan Tallon, F. Gerald Downing, and many others have urged the various meanings of faith in different contexts, even if it includes especially reliance on God.[26] Tallon regards faith in Paul as "intertwining trust, faithful obedience, trustworthiness, and more," while Chrysostom's handling of Pauline texts on faith, he says, provides "examples of [a] range of interpretive possibilities."[27] Downing asserts: "What is ruled out, then, it is here argued, is any hard precision, and clear lines, between possible connotations of particular words, the kind of 'nice' distinctions desired in some theological or ideological discourse."[28] Clearly, then, in Paul, let alone in the New Testament as a whole, faith is not one thing. Hampton, among others, shows how helpful the term "polymorphic" can be in education and teaching.[29]

The New Testament writers were aware that in the Old Testament the Hebrew word *'mn* ("firm, reliable, trustworthy") and its Hiphil grammatical form *he'ĕmîn* ("to trust in, have faith in") lie behind the New Testament uses of "faith" (*pistis*).[30] Thus Paul quotes Genesis 15:6 verbatim: Abraham "believed the LORD; and the LORD reckoned it to him as righteousness" (Rom. 4:3 NRSV). Parallels occur in Exodus 14:31: "The people . . . believed in the LORD" (NRSV); in Numbers 14:11: "How long will they refuse to believe in me?" (NRSV); and Deuteronomy 1:32: "You have no trust in the LORD your God" (NRSV). In other contexts the Hebrew noun *'ĕmet* may denote "security, fidelity, truth, and faithfulness."

---

26. Jonathan Tallon, "Faith in Paul: The View from Late Antiquity," paper delivered at the British New Testament Conference, Manchester, September 2014; F. Gerald Downing, "Ambiguity, Ancient Semantics, and Faith," *New Testament Studies* 56 (2010): 139–62.

27. Tallon, "Faith in Paul," 3, 7.

28. Downing, "Ambiguity, Ancient Semantics, and Faith," 156.

29. James A. Hampton, "Polymorphous Concepts in Semantic Memory," *Journal of Verbal Learning and Verbal Behavior* 18 (1979): 441–53.

30. Francis Brown, S. R. Driver, and C. A. Briggs (eds.), *Hebrew and English Lexicon of the Old Testament* (repr. Lafayette: Associated, 1980), 52–53.

The controversial interpretation of Habakkuk 2:4, "the righteous shall live by their faith," as Paul quotes it in Romans 1:17, provides a second reason why Bultmann cannot be accused of exaggeration. The hugely differing interpretation of faith in biblical passages underlines its various or polymorphic meanings. The Hebrew version of Habakkuk 2:4 has "his faith" (*be'ĕmûnātô*), which the Greek Septuagint translates as "my faith." Paul omits both possessive pronouns.[31] In the argument about whether Paul means "shall live by faith" (Cranfield and others) or "righteous by faith" (Leenhardt and others), James Dunn argues that Paul does not wish to exclude either. He comments: "When *pistis* [faith] is understood as *trust*, better sense can be made of *both* the chief alternative forms."[32] When the term is applied to God, the root *'mn* usually means "the faithful God." Artur Weiser concludes that uses of *'mn* are "fluid."[33] Problems of interpretation also occur in the famous phrase "the faith of Jesus Christ" (Greek *pistis Iēsou Christou*) in Galatians 3:22 and related passages. Richard Hays provides a meticulous discussion of the range of scholarly voices and interpretations in his masterly book *The Faith of Jesus Christ*.[34] Further, Michael Bird and P. M. Sprinkle edited a whole book of essays on the subject, and Don Garlington wrote a careful study on faith and obedience.[35]

To continue with extended uses of *pistis* in the broadly Pauline writings, it may sometimes denote "the faith" (e.g., Gal. 1:23; Eph. 4:5; Phil. 2:17; 1 Tim. 1:19; 3:9; 2 Tim. 4:7; and Tit. 3:15). Sometimes Paul may also speak of faith as a gift that is given to some Christians, but not all. The classic reference

31. For an extended discussion of the complex difficulties of interpretation, see R. W. L. Moberly, "'-m-n," in *New International Dictonary of Old Testament Theology and Exegesis*, ed. Willem A. VanGemeren (Carlisle: Paternoster, 1997), 1.425-33.

32. James D. G. Dunn, *Romans* (Dallas: Word, 1988), 1.45-46 (emphasis added).

33. Artur Weiser, "*Pisteuō*: The O.T. Concept," in *Theological Dictionary of the New Testament*, ed. G. Kittel (Grand Rapids: Eerdmans, 1968), 6.182-96 at 196.

34. Richard B. Hays, *The Faith of Jesus Christ: The Narrative Substructure of Galatians 3:1–4:11*, Society of Biblical Literature Dissertation Series 56 (Atlanta: Scholars Press, 1983; repr. Grand Rapids: Eerdmans, 2002), esp. 156; cf. also Henrik Ljungman, *Pistis: Its Presuppositions and Meaning in Pauline Use* (Lund: Gleerup, 1964), 38-40.

35. Michael F. Bird and Preston M. Sprinkle (eds.), *The Faith of Jesus Christ: The Pistis Christou Debate* (Milton Keynes: Paternoster/Peabody, MA: Hendrickson, 2009); and Don Garlington, *Faith, Obedience, and Perseverance: Aspects of Paul's Letter to the Romans*, Wissenschaftliche Untersuchungen zum Neuen Testament 2/38 (Tübingen: Mohr, 1994; repr. Eugene, OR: Wipf & Stock, 2009).

here is 1 Corinthians 12:9, where it is a "gift of the Spirit." It cannot be justi-
fying faith or trust here, for all Christians are given this. It probably denotes
here a buoyant, confident faith in God's purposes for the church, especially
when it suffers discouraging times. This may be equivalent to a faith that can
move mountains (13:2). In the context of justification through faith, faith and
justification seem to be internally related, to denote appropriation of God's
promise. Only perhaps in 1 Corinthians 13, where Paul speaks of "faith, hope,
and love" does it possibly approach Aquinas's notion of faith as a virtue.

In the Synoptic Gospels some examples of faith occur in the triple tra-
dition, for example: "Your faith has made you well" (Matt. 9:22; Mark 5:34;
Luke 8:48). Faith occurs in the healing of the paralytic (Matt. 9:2; Mark 2:5).
Matthew and Luke recount the saying: "If your faith is the size of a mustard
seed" (Matt. 17:20; Luke 17:6). Here the term probably means "trust" and
commitment.

Only in James does faith amount to mere assent to general truths or
doctrine. James argues that faith must be evidenced by works (Jas. 2:22–26):
"You believe that God is one; you do well. Even the demons believe—and
shudder" (2:19 NRSV). He adds: Abraham's "faith was brought to completion
by the works" (2:22 NRSV). Joachim Jeremias shows that Paul and James
do not contradict each other, because the context and concept of faith are
different: James attacks a theoretical monotheism abstracted from action
and commitment; he is not opposing Paul.[36]

Probably the most famous definition of faith comes in the Epistle to the
Hebrews. The writer declares: "Now faith is the assurance [*hypostasis*] of
things hoped for, the conviction [*elenchos*] of things not seen" (11:1 NRSV).
Oscar Cullmann convincingly argues that "things not seen" are as much
temporal as spatial, that is, they are "not seen" because they have not yet
taken place; they belong to the future. He explains: "Primitive Christian faith
and thinking do not start from the spatial contrast between the Here and
the Beyond, but from the time distinction between Formerly and Now and
Then . . . Hebrews [11:1] names . . . 'things hoped for.'"[37] This corresponds
with Paul: "We look not at what can be seen but at what cannot be seen; for

---

36. Joachim Jeremias, "Paul and James," *Expository Times* 66 (1955): 368–71; and An-
thony C. Thiselton, *The Two Horizons* (Grand Rapids: Eerdmans, 1980), 422–27.
37. Oscar Cullmann, *Christ and Time* (London: SCM, 1951), 37.

what is seen can be temporary, but what cannot be seen is eternal" (2 Cor. 4:18 NRSV); and, "We walk by faith, not by sight" (5:7 NRSV). Yet Hebrews also regards faith as "belief that": "He who comes to God must believe that he is" (Heb. 11:6).

In Aquinas believing is less a state of mind than a disposition and habit. Faith is a "cognitive habit" that seeks the truth of God.[38] Martin Luther defined it as "a living, daring confidence in God's grace, so sure and certain that a man would stake his life on it a thousand times. This confidence in God's grace . . . makes men glad and bold and happy."[39] The dispositional character of faith is amply demonstrated by H. H. Price in his book *Belief*. Belief, he declares, describes what the believer "would be likely to say or do or feel, if such and such circumstances were to arise. For example, he would assert the proposition [i.e., that God exists, or is active] . . . if he heard someone else denying it, or expressing doubt of it."[40] If it were merely a conscious state of mind, we might be tempted to deny that a believer still believed if he fell asleep or was knocked unconscious. Aquinas and Locke also discuss faith and reason extensively, as I consider further below.

No easy or simple system of classifications of the meanings of faith can readily be made. The meanings of faith vary in accordance with their context; in technical terms, "faith" is polymorphous. I shall consider thirteen possible meanings in accordance with context, although Moberly appears to suggest fifteen:

1. Faith is "belief that," for example, the proposition "that God exists" (Heb. 11:6).
2. Faith motivates action, as when "by faith Abraham obeyed when he was called to set out" from his land (Heb. 11:8).
3. Faith stands in contrast to sight (or to the present), that is, is directed toward "things hoped for" (Heb. 11:1; 2 Cor. 4:18; 5:7).
4. In entirely formal terms, faith is reduced to mere assent to *the* faith or orthodoxy (Eph. 4:5, 13; 1 Tim. 1:2; 4:1).
5. Faith is virtually equivalent to appropriation of grace and salvation, in-

38. Thomas Aquinas, *Summa Theologiae* (Oxford: Blackfriars, 1963), §2.2 Q1 arts. 1, 7.
39. Martin Luther, cited in E. G. Rupp and B. Drewery, *Martin Luther* (London: Arnold, 1970), 95.
40. H. H. Price, *Belief* (London: Allen & Unwin, 1969), 20.

volving trust in God's promises "on the basis of faith" (*ek pisteōs*; e.g., Rom. 1:17).

6. Faith involves believing in (*ho pisteuōn eis auton*; e.g., John 3:16) and is characteristic of the Johannine writings, for example, "on the basis of faith" (*ek pisteōs*; e.g., Rom. 1:17; cf. Hab. 2:4; Gal. 3:11).

7. Faith is a continuous, moment-by-moment habit or disposition, as in John's "abiding" (John 15:4) and probably in Paul's "through faith for faith" (Rom. 1:17).

8. Faith is a special gift to an individual only, but for the sake of the church (1 Cor. 12:9).

9. One can ask for an increased degree of faith (Luke 17:5).

10. Faith denotes "the faith" (e.g., Gal. 1:23; Eph. 4:5; Phil. 2:17; 1 Tim. 1:19).

11. Faith shades into faithfulness, as Moberly and N. T. Wright show (Rom. 1:8; Gal. 3:23).

12. Faith's relation to reason is debated (cf. Heb. 11:6–7; Acts 14:27; Rom. 10:8), with Aquinas and Calvin stressing their compatibility, and Tertullian and Kierkegaard arguing for the opposite. Kierkegaard defines it as "a wonder."[41]

13. "The obedience of faith" occurs in a context in Romans 1:5 and 16:26.

This list is not exhaustive. It simply proves the case about the various meanings of faith in the Bible and in historical theology. It is a polymorphous concept.[42] It perhaps reflects what Wittgenstein calls "a complicated network of similarities overlapping and crisscrossing: . . . I can think of no better expression to characterize these similarities than 'family resemblances.'"[43]

The Various Meanings of Certainty

Examination of certainty has to begin with two different approaches. On one level, I must evaluate evidence of the meaning of certainty in the New Testament texts. From another point of view, it is also important to try to

41. Søren Kierkegaard, *Philosophical Fragments* (Princeton: Princeton University Press, 1985), 65.

42. Cf. BDAG 816–21.

43. Wittgenstein, *Philosophical Investigations* §§66–67.

tackle complex philosophical discussions of certainty, including those of many thinkers from René Descartes and John Locke to Ludwig Wittgenstein and Alvin Plantinga in more recent thought. Different contexts such as law, medicine, history, natural sciences, social sciences, and Christian faith radically dictate what we may think of as certainty.

At first sight each of these approaches underlines my contention that certainty is no less various in meaning (or polymorphous) than doubt and faith. On the biblical side the problem is compounded by the variety of synonyms through which biblical writers express certainty. Louw and Nida define Greek *bebaios* as "known to be true, certain, verified" (Heb. 2:2; Mark 16:20).[44] Its frequency in this sense is relatively rare. A more typical example is Greek *asphaleia* and *asphalēs*, which Louw and Nida define as "certainty, being without doubt" (Luke 1:4; Acts 21:34; 22:30; 25:26; Heb. 6:19).[45] Often the word means "safe," especially in Classical Greek. In Philippians 3:1 the NRSV renders the term "safeguard": "To write the same things . . . for you it is a safeguard"; while KJV translates this word simply as "safe." Louw and Nida suggest that *plērophoreō* and *plērophoria* mean "to be absolutely sure, to be certain, complete certainty" (Rom. 4:21; 1 Thess. 1:5).[46] They classify *peithō* ("to be convinced, persuaded") in the same way (Rom. 8:38-39; Luke 16:31; Phil. 1:6).[47] In its adverbial form Greek *ontōs* means "really, actually."[48]

In their main section, Louw and Nida include *pantōs* ("altogether, certainly, doubtless"; Acts 21:22; 28:4) and *pistos* ("sure"; Acts 13:34).[49] They also include *kalōs* ("certainly, very well"; Acts 25:10) and the discourse marker *eulogōn eulogēsō* as a Hebraism ("I will certainly bless you") and *idou* ("look!" in the sense of "indeed").[50] These are simply markers of emphasis. Danker and Thayer broadly confirm these meanings. A concordance study would confirm this range of Greek and English meanings, including "sure," in the biblical writers' various vocabulary denoting certainty.

A very different approach to certainty is the philosophical one. Multiple

44. Johannes P. Louw and Eugene A. Nida (eds.), *Greek-English Lexicon of the New Testament Based on Semantic Domains* (New York: United Bible Societies, 1989), 1.340.
45. Ibid., 1.371.
46. Ibid., 1.371.
47. Ibid., 1.371-72.
48. Ibid., 1.667.
49. Ibid., 1.670.
50. Ibid., 1.687, 811-12.

meanings abound in philosophy. Peter D. Klein, one of the few authors to write an entire book on certainty, declares: "'Certainty' is not a univocal concept" (i.e., a concept that has one, single, uniform, meaning).[51]

Traditionally it is customary to distinguish between psychological or subjective certainty (especially of people) and objective, logical, or propositional certainty (especially of propositions). Psychological certainty denotes a full and intense conviction on the part of those who claim to be certain about something. It is synonymous with confidence or being completely convinced. But John Locke (1632–1704) argued that sheer intensity of conviction is no proof whatever of the truth of the belief or that it is "from God."[52] He explains: "St Paul believed that he did well and that he had a call to it when he *persecuted the Christians*."[53] In broader terms, Nicholas Wolterstorff shows that whereas many philosophers focus on Locke's books 1–3 (mainly about the empirical basis of human knowledge and the rejection of "innate ideas"), book 4 contained a treasure of thought on faith and reason, especially what he called "a theory of *entitled . . .* belief."[54]

In contrast to psychological certainty, which generally has not greatly influenced philosophers, objective, logical, or propositional certainty takes two distinct forms. To a mathematician such as French philosopher René Descartes (1596–1650), it seemed obvious to compare "the multiplicity and diversity of human opinions" with the more positive "certainties" conveyed by mathematics and logic.[55] On human opinions he observed: "Nothing solid could have been built on such a shifting foundation."[56] His foundation in the search for knowing "clearly and distinctly" was the self-evident truths of the human mind, of which he formulated as beyond all doubt "I think, therefore I exist" (Latin *cogito, ergo sum*).[57] But if we are to doubt the clarity

---

51. Peter D. Klein, "Certainty," in *Routledge Encyclopaedia of Philosophy*, ed. Edward Craig (London: Routledge, 1998), 2.264–67 at 264; and idem, *Certainty: A Refutation of Scepticism* (Minneapolis: University of Minnesota Press, 1981).

52. John Locke, *An Essay concerning Human Understanding* (Oxford: Clarendon, 1979 [orig. 1689]), 4.19.

53. Ibid., 4.19.12 (emphasis added).

54. Nicholas Wolterstorff, *John Locke and the Ethics of Belief* (Cambridge: Cambridge University Press, 1996), xv (emphasis added).

55. René Descartes, *Discourse on Method* (London: Penguin, 1968), 33.

56. Ibid., 32.

57. Ibid., 4.53.

and certainty of every proposition based on experience, certainty seems to apply only to the assertions of logic. In technical terms, philosophers call these "logically necessary propositions," in contrast to "contingent propositions." Contingent propositions are usually applicable to everyday life, whereas logically necessary ones are abstracted from human life and dictated by logic or the mind alone. I consider the pseudocertainty of such necessary or analytical propositions in part 3.

Wittgenstein often called necessary propositions merely internal or formal propositions. They have currency only within the self-evident domains of logic or mathematics. There could be no doubt that the three angles of a triangle amount to 180°, or that water boils at 100° C, because these are the very definitions of triangles or boiling point. The practical problem seems to be that these propositions are circular: they are true by definition, or by logical necessity. Wittgenstein observes: "What sort of proposition is this: 'We *cannot* have a miscalculation in 12 x 12 = 144'? It must surely be a proposition of logic."[58] In *Philosophical Investigations* he considers such propositions as "every rod has a length," "this body has extension," or "one plays patience by oneself," to which one can reply only "of course."[59] Such assertions are virtually equivalent to tautologies, or to analytical statements. They simply express what is true by definition. In *On Certainty* he explains that they do not engage with everyday life.

The circularity of what Wittgenstein calls analytical propositions suggests to Wittgenstein a third type of certainty: "All testing, all confirmation of a hypothesis takes place already within a system."[60] A child, to begin with, believes a host of things, and "bit by bit there forms a system of what is believed, and in that system some things stand *unshakeably fast*, and some . . . shift. *What stands fast* . . . is held fast by what lies around it."[61] Propositions that "stand fast" are "like the axis around which a body rotates."[62] Wittgenstein adds: "What I hold fast is not *one* proposition but a *nest of propositions*."[63] He concludes: "Isn't this 'certainty' already *presupposed* in the

---

58. Ludwig Wittgenstein, *On Certainty* (Oxford: Blackwell, 1969), §43.
59. Wittgenstein, *Philosophical Investigations* §§248, 251, 252.
60. Wittgenstein, *On Certainty* §105.
61. Ibid., §145 (emphasis added).
62. Ibid., §152.
63. Ibid., §225.

language-game? Something must be taught to us as a foundation."[64] These self-evident propositions are like hinges on which other propositions turn.

Wittgenstein is not arguing that presuppositions of this kind guarantee certainty. He expounds a second form of nonsubjective certainty simply because it exposes the arbitrary assumption of G. E. Moore on sheer commonsense knowledge or certainty in a purely theoretical or abstract way. For our purposes it exposes the various and complex nature of certainty. Wittgenstein does not identify certainty with knowledge.[65] In this light, we may return again to consider certainty in the New Testament. For the present, this discussion of Wittgenstein's *On Certainty* is provisional, for it remains controversial, with many differing interpretations. On what basis, we may ask, are the New Testament writers fully convinced or persuaded, apart from the merely subjective or psychological state of conviction and belief? Or do they, in the end, rely simply on subjective certainty? Perhaps finite, fallible, human beings cannot expect certainty, unless by revelation from God.

The distinction between subjective and objective certainty remains important both for the New Testament writings and philosophy. But in the New Testament the two may overlap. One striking and well-known example comes in Romans 8:38-39: "For I am convinced [perhaps persuaded, based on perfect *pepeismai* with present force] that neither death nor life . . . nor anything else in all creation will be able to separate us from the love of God that is in Christ Jesus our Lord" (NIV; NRSV is similar). Fitzmyer comments: "Paul adds his personal conviction as the conclusion to the hymn"; his statement is a first-person singular one.[66] In this sense, it includes subjective certainty. Nevertheless, as N. T. Wright rightly comments, this comes at the conclusion of a careful argument and is introduced by "for" (Greek *gar*): "The final *gar* of this section explains the shout of triumph in terms of [a] settled conviction." He explains at once that the "settled conviction" is grounded "on what Paul knows about the Messiah, Jesus, the Lord."[67] It also takes account of the one true God's pouring out the Holy Spirit and his generous love through Jesus. Paul's warrant or grounding for his psychological

---

64. Ibid., §§446, 449.

65. Klein, *Certainty*, 117–18.

66. Joseph A. Fitzmyer, *Romans*, Anchor Bible 33 (New York: Doubleday, 1992), 534.

67. N. T. Wright, "The Letter to the Romans," in *New Interpreter's Bible*, ed. Leander Keck (Nashville: Abingdon, 2002), 10.614.

certainty is the argument from Romans 5:1 to 8:39, which concludes with the expression of logical, objective, or propositional certainty: "Nothing can separate us from the love of God in Christ Jesus our Lord." This grounding is not a single proposition, but a "nest of propositions" that are interrelated. Anders Nygren comments: "In all the uncertainty that marks this earthly life, there is still something which is absolutely fixed and certain, namely, God's election and Christ's love."[68]

Paul also uses *peithō* in Philippians 1:6: "I am confident ... that [*pepoithōs ... hoti*] the one who began a good work among you will bring it to completion by the day of Jesus Christ" (NRSV). This similarly combines personal subjective certainty with an objective certainty grounded on a host of propositions about God, Christ, salvation, redemption, and God's purposes. It could not be reduced to a single proposition. In Philippians 3:1, however, he uses the Greek word *asphalēs*: "To write the same things to you is not troublesome to me, and for you it is a safeguard [*asphalēs*]" (NRSV). Danker translates this as "a safe course," although normally, he says, it means what "ensures certainty."[69] The Greek noun *asphaleia* is thus used more typically in Luke 1:4: "So that you may know the truth" (NRSV). The NIV translates: "So that you may know the certainty of the things you have been taught," and NJB renders the word "well founded." Danker suggests that the passage expresses both "certainty" and "truth," with the notions of stability and security in the background.[70] In Hebrews 2:2, *bebaios* also conveys certainty. The NRSV renders it: "The message declared through angels was valid." NJB translates the word "reliable." Danker accepts both meanings. It is "something that can be relied upon" and "have validity," as well as being "beyond doubt."[71]

These examples are hardly simply psychological certainty. They are grounded in a multiplicity of propositions, all of which place the certainty beyond individual subjectivity. Whether these constitute an adequate ground or warrant remains to be considered in part 3. Nothing, however, can hide the variable meanings of certainty. Like doubt and faith, it is also a polymorphous concept and varies in meaning from context to context.

68. Anders Nygren, *Commentary on Romans* (London: SCM, 1952), 348.
69. BDAG 147.
70. BDAG 147.
71. BDAG 172.

PART I

DOUBT

CHAPTER 2

Doubt and Skepticism

Ancient Greek Skepticism

It is tempting to think of the influential period of skepticism as beginning with Pyrrhon of Elis (ca. 365–ca. 275 BC), in effect the founder of the skeptic school. Later he was notably followed by Sextus Empiricus (ca. 250–325 AD). The Greek word *skeptikos* originally meant "inquirer." Pyrrhon, however, wrote nothing, and the high point of skepticism is more appropriately associated with the period of the Renaissance, when the texts of Sextus were rediscovered. They were often used by some in the Roman Catholic Church, supposedly to undermine appeals by Luther and Protestantism to the biblical and rational basis of their confidence.[1]

Most skeptics from the time of the ancient Greeks onward question whether any probable or certain knowledge can be gained about reality. But the scope and degree of skepticism vary, and the term "skepticism" can denote various meanings. Pyrrhon had been taught by Anaxarchus, a follower of Democritus, and joined the entourage of Alexander the Great as court philosopher. He therefore inherited the atomist philosophy of Democritus, which regarded reality as composed of indivisible physical particles, and sense-perceptions as often contradicting one another. According to a life of Pyrrhon written by Diogenes Laërtius, Pyrrhon's skepticism led him to sit

---

1. See especially Richard H. Popkin, *The History of Scepticism from Erasmus to Spinoza* (Berkeley: University of California Press, 1979).

loose to all commonsense perceptions. Supposedly his friends several times preserved him from death by walking off a precipice, by being run down by a cart, or by being savaged by a wild dog. But many reject such stories and understand his skepticism simply as a questioning tool for debate, in the tradition of Socrates's use of questions and doubts. He is said to have appealed to *isosthenia*, or the balancing of opposing views, in such a way that each canceled out the other. In the absence of any firm belief, he felt free to practice tranquility and detachment.[2]

Although traditionally Pyrrhon is thought of as the founder of skepticism, long before Pyrrhon some Greek philosophers held elements of skepticism. Xenophanes of Colophon (ca. 570–500 BC) made a series of attacks on the Olympic pantheon of deities, producing satires on their anthropomorphic characteristics. In his writings he declared that no criterion of true knowledge exists, whether about the gods or other matters.[3] Human beings, he said, can have no certain knowledge, only opinions.

In the late fifth century BC Gorgias and especially Protagoras were well known for their relativism. Gorgias argued that nothing exists, and that if it did, it still could not be known, let alone be communicated. Protagoras (ca. 490–ca. 420 BC), the most eminent of the Sophists, became notorious for his maxim "man is the measure of all things, of things that are, that they are, and of things that are not, that they are not."[4] In other words, he espoused relativism and subjectivism. He insisted on theological agnosticism: "I am unable to know either that deities exist or that they do not exist."[5]

In the third century BC the leaders of Plato's Academy rejected Plato's metaphysics and over-pressed the remark attributed to Socrates: "All that I know is that I know nothing." The context of these Socratic dialogues, however, had been to distinguish knowledge from opinion. Hence these more skeptical philosophers were often called "the New Academy." From this tradition came Carneades (ca. 213–128 BC) and Aenesidemus (first century BC). Aenesidemus founded his skepticism on the different appearance of things.

2. Cf. Norman MacColl, *The Greek Sceptics from Pyrrho to Sextus* (London: Forgotten Books, 1869; repr. 2012).

3. Xenophanes, *Fragments* 34.

4. Protagoras, *Fragments* 1.

5. Protagoras, *Fragments* 4. Cf. W. K. C. Guthrie, *The Sophists* (Cambridge: Cambridge University Press, 1971; a reprint of vol. 3 of his *History of Greek Philosophy*).

If things can seem so different under different conditions, how could we be certain that we know them for what they are? Much later Sextus Empiricus was regarded as the codifier of Greek skepticism. Later still came Diogenes Laërtius (AD 300–350). Meanwhile in the first century BC, Marcus Tullius Cicero (a well-known rhetorician) was primarily a judicious Roman statesman who radically opposed dogmatism. His critical insights, therefore, led at times to partial skepticism.

Sextus had been a careful student of the history of skepticism in Greece and produced extensive writings. Among his many claims to fame (or notoriety) he saw that the New Academy virtually undermined their supposed skepticism by being "sure" of their skepticism, that is, that they could not know truth or reality. He saw the dilemma that if a person claims to know nothing, how can he or she know that they cannot know? The position is that of philosophical agnosticism. Sextus "solved" this perceived contradiction by replacing the dogmatic assertion "we cannot know" simply with suspense of judgment. We can speak of "appearances," he acknowledged, but must remain silent about knowledge of reality. In the event, his writings fall into two groups: *Hypotyposes* ("Outlines of Pyrrhonism") and *Adversus Mathematicos* ("Against the Dogmatists"). Sextus attacked especially the dogmatism of the Stoics. He even argued that the use of Aristotle's logical syllogism was merely circular. For example, the conclusion "Socrates is mortal" is presupposed by the major premise "all men are mortal." In *Against the Dogmatists*, Plato, Aristotle, Zeno, and Epictetus were all categorized as Dogmatists. Sextus even remained silent about probabilities. Like Pyrrhon, Sextus held the practical aim of *tranquility* (Greek *ataraxia*).[6] At very least from the Greek period we may draw the basic paradox of true skepticism that to claim to know that we do not know would be self-contradictory! We can only suspend a growing number of claims to believe.

6. Cf. R. G. Bury, *Sextus Empiricus*, Loeb Classical Library (London: Heineman, 1917–55); Mary Mills Patrick, *Sextus Empiricus and Greek Scepticism* (Cambridge: Cambridge University Press, 1899); and idem, *Sextus Empiricus: Outlines of Scepticism*, ed. J. Annas and J. Barnes (Cambridge: Cambridge University Press, 1994).

Renaissance Skepticism

Richard Popkin asserts that "the Pyrrhonian view seems to have been almost unknown in the West until its discovery in the sixteenth century," while the view of the New Academy was known only through Augustine's refutation of it.[7] The next crucial period is 1500–1675, when "scepticism plays a different role in the period from the Reformation up to the formulation of the Cartesian philosophy."[8] Descartes's simultaneous "super-skepticism" (as many call it, especially in his "evil demon hypothesis") and his refutation of skepticism, Popkin continues, "made the sceptics turn their attack against his system instead of against their traditional opponents. Hence, the sceptical arguments had to be altered to fit the new opponent."[9]

The most radical effect of this transformation or reorientation, Popkin believes, is that in the changed situation "'sceptic' and 'believer' are not opposing classifications."[10] As he also observes, the skeptics of the sixteenth and seventeenth centuries were often sincere believers in the Christian religion, almost unanimously. It is not that they failed to believe, but they had doubts about the rational or evidential arguments for such beliefs. They were theists, but many were also fideists.[11] (Fideism, at its simplest, denotes the view that a system of religious beliefs cannot be tested by any criterion external to itself, including rational criteria. I return to the subject in a later discussion of Kierkegaard.) I should perhaps want cautiously to include Pascal and Kierkegaard under this heading, but Augustine, Luther, and Calvin can be called fideists only in the broadest sense that, as Popkin admits, in their case "reasons *can* be given for faith, *after* one has accepted it."[12] Strict fideism would suggest, in its more extreme form, as Kierkegaard does, that faith takes the form of self-contradiction and paradox. He explicitly uses the example of when Abraham was called to slay the son of promise (Gen. 22).[13]

7. Popkin, *History of Scepticism*, xvi.
8. Ibid., xvi.
9. Ibid., xviii.
10. Ibid., xix.
11. Ibid., xx.
12. Ibid.
13. Søren Kierkegaard, *Fear and Trembling* and *The Sickness unto Death* (Princeton: Princeton University Press, 1941), 98.

In the narrative of Abraham, he writes, faith is "the paradox which does not ✓ permit of mediation."[14]

Alvin Plantinga helpfully defines fideism as "the exclusive or basic reliance upon faith alone, accompanied by a consequent disparagement of reason," and urges "reliance on faith rather than reason."[15] In this sense, faith is independent of reason. Kierkegaard fits into this category. He writes, for example: "The object of faith is not a doctrine, for then the relationship would be intellectual. . . . Faith constitutes a sphere all by itself. . . . Every misunderstanding of Christianity may at once be recognized by . . . transferring it to the sphere of the intellectual."[16] Kierkegaard applies the principle not only to faith, but also to truth: "When subjectivity, inwardness, is the truth, the truth objectively defined becomes a paradox."[17] He adds: "Subjectivity is truth; subjectivity is reality."[18] "Subjectivity" here primarily has the meaning of being sharpened into an "I," who is deeply involved.

Thus, as is the case with doubt, faith, and certainty, Popkin concedes: "Fideism covers a range of possible views, extending from (i) that of blind faith, which denies any capacity whatsoever to reason to reach the truth . . . to (ii) that of making faith prior to reason."[19] On this basis probably Pascal and Kierkegaard would belong to the first category; Augustine and perhaps Calvin and Luther would belong to the second, although reason is important to Calvin.

All this sets the scene for skepticism from the Reformation to Descartes. Desiderius Erasmus (ca. 1466-1536) suggests "a kind of sceptical basis for remaining within the Catholic Church."[20] In his book *The Praise of Folly*, Erasmus insists: "Human affairs are so obscure and various that nothing can be clearly known. This was the sound conclusion of the Academics [i.e., the Academic Skeptics]."[21] He dedicated his book to his friend Thomas More.

---

14. Kierkegaard, *Fear and Trembling*, 128.

15. Alvin Plantinga, "Reason and Belief in God," in *Faith and Rationality: Reason and Belief in God*, ed. Alvin Plantinga and Nicholas Wolterstorff (Notre Dame: University of Notre Dame Press, 1984), 87.

16. Søren Kierkegaard, *Concluding Unscientific Postscript* (Princeton: Princeton University Press, 1941), 291.

17. Ibid., 183.

18. Ibid., 306.

19. Popkin, *History of Scepticism*, xix.

20. Ibid., 5.

21. Desiderius Erasmus, *The Praise of Folly* (Chicago: Packard, 1946), 84.

Both Erasmus and More believed that such obscurity entirely undermined Luther and Zwingli's constant appeal to Scripture. It was against this background that Luther's doctrine of the "clarity" or "perspicuity" of Scripture was developed. This implied not that the Bible presented no problems at all of interpretation; after all, Calvin published numerous exegetical commentaries. On the other hand, as Luther and Calvin saw it, God had pointed through Scripture and reason enough that was clear to take the next step of faith.

It must not be forgotten that Erasmus was a distinguished scholar of the Greek New Testament, who taught divinity and New Testament studies at Cambridge, where he succeeded St. John Fisher as Lady Margaret's Professor and published his translation of the New Testament into Latin in Basel. He held in common with Luther his love of the New Testament and his reservations about scholasticism. However, Martin Luther (1483–1546) published first the *Heidelberg Catechism* and the *Leipzig Disputation* in 1519, and then after that *The Appeal to the German Nobility* and *The Babylonian Captivity of the Church*. These took the critical step of denying the authority of "the rule of faith" of the Catholic Church and the infallibility of the pope. Erasmus may have been sympathetic with Luther's earliest protest against papal authority. However, like Thomas More, he ultimately sought peace and reconciliation, in spite of Luther's earlier protests. Erasmus believed that Luther's later challenges to the authority of the church went too far. In 1524 he entered the Reformation controversy in his *Diatribe concerning Free Will*, in which he expressed disagreements with Luther. Luther replied to this, in his famous treatise *The Bondage of the Will* in 1525.

In his *Appeal to the German Nobility* (1521) Luther appealed to "the testimony of Scripture," to "the unsupported authority of the Pope," and to "manifest reasoning," concluding: "I stand convicted by the Scriptures ... and my conscience is taken captive by God's word. ... On this I take my stand."[22] This amounted to a denial of universally accepted criteria in the West and assumed the clarity of Scripture. Therefore, Popkin explains: "Erasmus's ... dislike of rational theological discussions led him to suggest a

---

22. Martin Luther, "Luther's Answer before the Emperor and the Diet of Worms, 18 April 1521," in *Martin Luther* by E. G. Rupp and Benjamin Drewery (London: Arnold, 1970), 60. It is difficult to verify the exact words. There appears to be no account in a firsthand source, although quotations occur numerous times in secondary literature.

kind of *sceptical basis for remaining within the Catholic Church.*"[23] As already noted, in *The Praise of Folly* Erasmus stated: "Human affairs are so obscure and various that nothing can clearly be known."[24]

James Atkinson, passionate advocate of Luther, indicates the sincerity of Erasmus's Christian belief in spite of his attack on Luther. In 1536 Erasmus was invited to become cardinal, but declined the honor. Atkinson writes: "He was a committed man . . . a sincere and enlightened believer in Christianity. . . . He never scoffed at religion. . . . Positively he sought to restore the Church to paths of biblical simplicity and spiritual purity. . . . He hated the vices and follies of monks and clergy, but still more their crass ignorance and gross superstition."[25] Nevertheless, Popkin asserts: "Erasmus was willing to admit that he could not tell with certainty what was true," although he was "willing to accept the decisions of the Church."[26] Popkin argues that this position is a non sequitur, and Luther pointed out that the Holy Spirit is not a skeptic, and insisted on certainty.

All the same, Popkin calls this view of the Reformers "subjective certainty" and "the compulsions of one's conscience."[27] The Catholic Church insisted that subjective certainty was no genuine certainty. Later, John Calvin (1509–64) would insist both that the testimony of the Spirit was self-validating and that this was not antirational. The debate widely continued. On the Catholic side Sebastian Castellio (1515–63) argued that much of Scripture is too opaque to allow any interpreter to be certain of the truth. On the Protestant side Theodore Beza (1519–1605), in effect Calvin's successor, attacked Castellio as simply reviving the New Academy.

Popkin concludes: "This type of attack finally led Protestant leaders to write tracts on the Pyrrhonism of the Church of Rome," arguing that we could never be sure on this basis "that the Church of Rome was the true Church."[28] David Boullier (1699–1759) of Amsterdam urged that the Catholic view introduced universal skepticism into the whole system of Christian reli-

---

23. Popkin, *History of Scepticism*, 5 (emphasis added).

24. Erasmus, *Praise of Folly*, 84.

25. James Atkinson, *Martin Luther and the Birth of Protestantism* (London: Penguin, 1968), 231.

26. Popkin, *History of Scepticism*, 7.

27. Ibid., 8.

28. Ibid., 13–14.

gion. Michel de Montaigne (1533–92) argued that the fallibility of the human mind meant that nothing can be known with certainty and that all judgment must be suspended. Popkin call de Montaigne "the most significant figure in the sixteenth century revival of ancient scepticism."[29] On the basis of Paul's denunciation of human wisdom in 1 Corinthians, Montaigne regarded truth as dependent on revelation and has often been called a fideist.[30]

In the seventeenth century, skepticism was somewhat mitigated and made more constructive. Martin Mersenne (1588–1648), a friend of Descartes, was trained at a Jesuit college and was known for his Christian piety. He argued on behalf of the "new science" and "the new philosophy" of Descartes, Galileo, Herbert of Cherbury, and others, and in 1625 Mersenne attacked the skepticism of Pyrrhon. In contrast to Pyrrhon, he argued that some things *are* known; for example, "there is a world." Some claim that Mersenne represented a halfway house between skepticism and dogmatism. Everything we know, he maintained, is open to some doubt. In comparison with Erasmus and with Pyrrhon and Sextus, Mersenne constitutes one more step in demonstrating varieties of skepticism.

Early Modern Skepticism

René Descartes (1596–1650) introduced a new era into philosophy. The climate of the times was to appeal to authorities and tradition for the quest for truth. But Descartes was a brilliant mathematician, within the limits of his day, and had scant regard for secondhand opinions gained from tradition and secondhand "authorities." The truths of mathematics and logic, he argued, could be discovered immediately and directly through the reasoning powers of the human mind. This method alone could lead to certainties. It could thereby also show the errors of skepticism.

Descartes was born in La Flèche, near Poitiers, and was educated in the Jesuit college of his hometown. He became friends with Mersenne in early years and became familiar with his views on the skepticism of Pyrrhon. His initial explanation of the method of mathematic and logic occurred in *Rules*

---

29. Ibid., 42.
30. Ibid., 49.

for the Direction of Mind. By this method some propositions could become self-evident and independent of other people's opinions. Thereby one could know completely. In effect anticipating Wittgenstein's *Tractatus*, Descartes's rule 5 expounded the method of reducing an obscure and complex proposition to simpler ones, and ultimately to the simplest. His method was deductive. Descartes had not yet formulated his dualism and believed that the "facts" of science could be included within such propositions, but unlike the *Tractatus*, treated facts of logic as facts of the sciences in the same way. Descartes's two later works, *Discourse on Method* (1637) and *The Meditations* (1641), are philosophical classics that have enjoyed enormous influence in Western philosophy and culture.[31]

In part 1 of *A Discourse on Method* Descartes recalls how, in his words, "I was given to believe by their help [i.e., literature and books] a clear and certain knowledge . . . might be acquired. But I . . . completely changed my mind."[32] He continues: "There is not a single matter . . . which is not in dispute . . . nothing [is] above doubt. . . . When I considered the number of conflicting opinions . . . I resolved no longer to seek any other science than the knowledge of myself."[33] Thus part 1 of the *Discourse* rehearses many of the traditional arguments of the skeptics.

In part 2 of his *Discourse*, Descartes considers how to dismantle a system that yielded uncertain knowledge. He comments: "I thought I could not do better than resolve at once to sweep them [traditional arguments] wholly away."[34] He is concerned, however, that not every person should "strip one's self of all past beliefs"; yet on the other hand "the ground of our opinions is far more [due to] custom and example than any certain knowledge."[35] In the end, he writes in *Meditation* 2 that he must "proceed by casting aside all that admits of the slightest doubt."[36] Such wholesale demolition should be undertaken only "once in a lifetime."[37]

In *Discourse* 4 Descartes provides his most memorable, often-repeated,

---

31. Descartes, *A Discourse on Method* (London: Dent, 1912/Penguin, 1968 [orig. 1637]); and *The Meditations* (Chicago: Open Court, 1901).
32. Descartes, *Discourse on Method* (Dent), 5.
33. Descartes, *Method* (Dent), 8; (Penguin), 33.
34. Ibid., 12.
35. Ibid., 12, 14.
36. Descartes, *Meditations*, 29.
37. Ibid., 33.

formulation: "This truth, *I think hence I am* [Latin *cogito ergo sum*] was so certain and of such evidence that no ground of doubt . . . could be alleged."[38] This constitutes the first principle of the philosophy for which he had been searching. In *Meditation 3* he expounds the phrase "I think." He explains: "I am a thinking (conscious) thing, that is a being who doubts, affirms, denies, knows a few objects."[39] He has discovered "what is essential to the truth and certainty of a proposition."[40] In part 5 of his *Discourse* he considers what may be deduced from this, including God, body and soul, and other entities, but reserves such discussion for elsewhere. The general effect is to attack skepticism. In part 6 he reemphasizes his argument, including the status of a priori truths, as against a posteriori inferences from opinions.

Descartes's *Meditation 5* goes further. He considers both matter and the existence of God. He formulates, in effect, a version of the ontological argument for the existence of God: "I cannot conceive a God unless as existing, any more than I can a mountain from that of a valley."[41] This gives the game away about his notion of supposed certainty. Existing is virtually presupposed by God, just as logically mountains cannot be what they are without valleys. Certainty is not simply abstract logical coherence, such as "a triangle amounts to two right angles, or the sum of its angles 180°." (I consider this further below under "Pseudocertainty in Analytical Statements," pp. 110–13.) This kind of supposed certainty is true in mathematics or logic, but leaves its role in life undetermined. Descartes adds: "It is in truth necessary to admit that God exists, after having supposed him to possess all perfections."[42] He then adds geometrical illustrations involving quadrilaterals, the rhombus, and so on. But, as Kant and later Bertrand Russell demonstrate, existence is not a predicate. Russell's existential quantifier exposes what most regard as the fallacy in Descartes's argument.

In *Meditation 6* Descartes opens himself to yet more criticism. He considers mind and body, which prompts the caricature of his dualism, made famous by Gilbert Ryle, of "the ghost in the machine." Descartes drew too sharp a distinction between the empirical realm of matter and the world of thought or ideas, as Plato had done. Ryle (1900–1976) was Waynflete Profes-

---

38. Descartes, *Method* (Dent), 26–27 (emphasis original).
39. Descartes, *Meditations*, 42.
40. Descartes, *Method*, 27.
41. Descartes, *Meditations*, 78.
42. Ibid., 79.

sor at Oxford and attacked Descartes's mind-body dualisms in his celebrated book *The Concept of the Mind*. He refers to Descartes's view of the body-mind relationship as "the official doctrine" and to the Cartesian view "with deliberate abuse" as "the dogma of the ghost in the machine. . . . It is one big mistake."[43] He attacks this as a "category mistake," as if "the body and mind are ordinarily harnessed together."[44] Ryle entertainingly considers "category mistake" with homely examples, such as "she came home in a flood of tears and a sedan chair."[45] It is as if the body were a mechanical engine, and the mind a controller or pilot, who directs the mind, as if by levers. Ryle insists: "There occur mental processes" does not mean the same sort of thing as "there occur physical processes." It is as if "a rising tide" could be coupled with "rising hopes."[46] The two are not "two collateral histories."

A number of other philosophers also attacked Descartes's views. J. L. Watling, for example, argues that "I think, therefore I am" is "not a statement at all, true or false"; it is a personal expression in which the second term is *presupposed* in the first. In the end, it is a circular statement of logical explication.[47] Popkin declares: "Descartes, having presented his triumphant conquest of the sceptical dragon, immediately found himself denounced as a dangerous Pyrrhonist, and as an unsuccessful dogmatist whose theories were only fantasies and illusions."[48] Critics who accepted the argument of the *First Meditation* regarded the later meditations as a "doubtful non sequitur." Calvin, among others, did not regard Descartes as establishing religious truth. The Jesuit Pierre Bourdin (who engaged in controversy with Descartes in 1639–40) complained that the method of Descartes "takes away our previous instruments, nor does it bring any to occupy their place."[49] Descartes protested against Bourdin's criticisms, but Popkin concludes: "There was no way and no hope of ever emerging from the sceptical despair that Descartes had introduced."[50]

43. Gilbert Ryle, *The Concept of the Mind* (London: Hutchinson, 1949), 17.
44. Ibid., 11.
45. Ibid., 23.
46. Ibid., 24.
47. J. L. Watling, "Descartes," in *A Critical History of Western Philosophy*, ed. D. J. O'Connor (London: Collier-Macmillan, 1964), 170–86 at 177.
48. Popkin, *History of Scepticism*, 193.
49. Cited in ibid., 195–96.
50. Ibid., 199.

In addition to Ryle, Watling, and Popkin, Paul Ricoeur, William Temple, and Helmut Thielicke also criticize the *cogito* of Descartes. In general terms these all attack Descartes's privileging of human consciousness. Ricoeur (1913–2005) declares about his anthropocentric confidence in human consciousness: "Since Marx, Nietzsche, and Freud, however, we may doubt even this."[51] In his later book *Oneself as Another*, Ricoeur also addresses the deceit of Descartes's supposed demons, which make "seeming" pass for "true being."[52] The Cartesian argument of the "evil genius" becomes a ground for claiming "the deceitful character of all language."[53] It paves the way for Nietzsche's skepticism: "Everything that reaches our consciousness is utterly ... adjusted [and] simplified."[54] Ricoeur's writings reflect a careful balance between suspicion and trust. He declares, for example, that "hermeneutics seems to me to be animated by this double motivation: willingness to suspect, willingness to listen; vow of rigour, vow of obedience. In our time ... we have barely begun to listen to symbols."[55]

Temple and Thielicke are theological critics of Descartes. William Temple (1881–1944) was Archbishop of Canterbury and greatly concerned with education and social work. He was first trained as a philosopher. His major critique of Descartes was his pretentious individualism. He seemed to place the individual self at the center of knowledge. Temple therefore wrote, in view of Descartes's great influence, that his reflection on himself in solitude was probably "the most disastrous moment in the history of Europe. ... Many of our worst troubles, not only in philosophy, but also in politics and economics ... are closely associated with the habit of thought then established"; it was "the Cartesian faux-pas."[56] The mistake was both human centeredness and especially individualism.

Helmut Thielicke (1908–86) stood in the Lutheran tradition and was primarily an ethicist. He emphatically condemned Descartes's anthropocentric approach, as if to suggest that humankind and human thinking are the

---

51. Paul Ricoeur, "A Philosophical Interpretation of Freud," in *The Conflict of Interpretations: Essays in Hermeneutics* (Evanston: Northwestern University Press, 1974), 148.

52. Paul Ricoeur, *Oneself as Another* (Chicago: University of Chicago Press, 1992), 6.

53. Ibid., 12.

54. Ibid., 14.

55. Paul Ricoeur, *Freud and Philosophy: An Essay on Interpretation* (New Haven: Yale University Press, 1970), 27.

56. William Temple, *Nature, Man, and God* (London: Macmillan, 1940), 57.

be-all and end-all of truth. Descartes might well have responded that he had defended belief in God and the Catholic faith, but Thielicke sees his legacy in these human-centered terms. Consciousness suffers criticism as a starting point also from such philosophers as Hans-Georg Gadamer and those thinkers who have seen the problem differently since Nietzsche and Freud.[57] In theological terms, many regard the self as too damaged and distorted by human sin to bear the weight that Descartes placed upon it. As Popkin suggests, although Descartes saw himself as a conqueror of skepticism, many critics see the *reverse*: his certainty is a pseudocertainty, and in the end he encourages skepticism.

A Moral and Social Case against Skepticism

W. Jay Wood in his book *Epistemology: Becoming Intellectually Virtuous* suggests our subheading.[58] Sometimes, he says, lack of belief or lack of knowledge may arise from such traits as gullibility, wilful naïveté, laziness, closed-mindedness, or intellectual dishonesty. This is not always the case, but it arises sufficiently frequently to demonstrate that there is sometimes a moral dimension to a person's skepticism. This aspect has often been unduly neglected. The reverse may be the case about the acquisition of knowledge or belief. What Wood calls "intellectual virtues" may include such qualities as "wisdom, prudence, foresight, understanding, discernment, truthfulness, and studiousness."[59] Such virtues may often constitute a more decisive influence on acquiring knowledge than simply a high IQ score. Wood speaks of "the two-way causal connection between right thinking and right morality," while in epistemology, he says, "your very character, the kind of person you are . . . is at stake."[60]

Whether someone is attentive, wise, discerning, prudent, teachable, humble, and tenacious may well be closely related to their intellectual life

57. Hans-Georg Gadamer, *Truth and Method*, 2nd ed. (London: Sheed & Ward, 1989), 19–30, 244–46, 271–85, 341–79.

58. W. Jay Wood, *Epistemology: Becoming Intellectually Virtuous* (Leicester: Apollos/ Downers Grove: IVP, 1998).

59. Ibid., 16.

60. Ibid., 17.

and belief system. Different virtues may relate to the acquisition of knowl-
edge from those that we will require for its maintenance. The acquisition
of knowledge suggests that we need eagerness to learn, being attentive and
observant, and being inquisitive. To maintain a belief system may require
tenacity, willingness to think through counterarguments, and so on. Often
it may also require an ability to distinguish genuine wisdom from the mere
gathering of information. There are limits, for example, to what sheer quan-
tification or computer-generated information can provide. Some of us may
lament the substitution of "information services" for "library," when the two
are not at all synonyms. The library may be a treasure store of judgments and
evaluations, many of them corporate.

Dru Johnson seems to go further still in his *Biblical Knowing*.[61] He
agrees that in the biblical writings knowledge is much more than informa-
tion. He begins with the very early biblical reference to "the knowledge of
good and evil" (Gen. 3:5). Belief arises not always from evidence, but from
"epistemic assent."[62] Following Kierkegaard, Johnson argues: "'Learning
Christ' is not just learning principles or maxims, rather it is transforma-
tive."[63] He appeals especially to Murray Rae's interpretation of Kierkegaard
in his *Kierkegaard's Vision of the Incarnation*.[64] Rae regards moral repen-
tance as part of this transformation. Like Wittgenstein, Johnson regards
"a mistake" as different from "being in error."[65] Error is not, he argues,
due to insufficient information.[66] He further appeals to Polanyi's *Personal
Knowledge*, which I consider later. On this basis it is not surprising that he
regards knowledge as involving participation, not the supposedly objective
role of the spectator.[67]

In the climax of his book, Johnson speaks of submission to voices be-
yond the self and the social dimension of knowledge. Christians find this
in the church. Johnson writes: "The epistemological goal is not merely in-

61. Dru Johnson, *Biblical Knowing: A Scriptural Epistemology of Error* (Eugene, OR: Cas-
cade Books, 2013).
62. Ibid., 5.
63. Ibid., 9.
64. Murray A. Rae, *Kierkegaard's Vision of the Incarnation: By Faith Transformed* (Oxford:
Oxford University Press, 1998).
65. Johnson, *Biblical Knowing*, 11.
66. Ibid., 20.
67. Ibid., 202.

dividual but is social as well."[68] In the case of Christian believers, Johnson cites the epistemological role of the teacher and preacher,[69] a point I make broadly later in this chapter.

While the moral dimension remains important, we should also avoid ascribing all doubt and skepticism to moral inadequacy. It is merely a factor that enters the picture in some or many cases, but certainly not in all cases.

The distinction between wisdom and information, however, is universally applicable.[70] In the Old Testament, wisdom helps us to cope with complexities in practical life. It is associated with corporate tradition and education, as seen in the transgenerational transmission of wisdom and knowledge. In the Old Testament there are nearly two hundred uses of "wisdom" (Hebrew *ḥokmâ*) and its cognate forms. They are mostly found in the three main wisdom books of Proverbs, Job, and Ecclesiastes and in the Jewish writings, especially the Wisdom of Solomon and Sirach. Hebrew does, however, use other terms to mean "understanding": *tĕbûnâ* and *bînâ*. Wisdom above all derives from the community, as well as from God, often over generations, whereas knowledge concerns primarily the individual. In Proverbs wisdom is typically passed on from parents: "My child, be attentive to my wisdom" (Prov. 5:1 NRSV). R. N. Whybray speaks of it as a "process of practical reasoning."[71] In ethical terms wisdom is associated with such moral qualities as humility (11:2), willingness to learn (21:5), and patience (14:29). Today this distinction between academic knowledge and communal, moral, practical, God-orientated wisdom is more crucial than ever for modern culture. Knowledge, as such, in a computerized, electronic age is often seen as sheer information. This may be available instantly, at the touch of a fingertip, without effort. Wisdom, by contrast, takes time and training, may depend on tradition, and may involve ethical dispositions. Wisdom relates to how we use information.

Descartes conceived of knowledge as primarily the work of the individual. Although this became the dominant tradition, Giambattista Vico (1668–1744) and Hans-Georg Gadamer (1900–2002) represent a different

68. Ibid., 209.
69. Ibid., 210.
70. Anthony C. Thiselton, "Wisdom in the New Testament," *Theology* 115 (2011): 163–72; and idem, "Wisdom in the Hebrew Bible and Judaism," *Theology* 114 (2011): 260–68.
71. R. N. Whybray, *Wisdom in Proverbs* (London: SCM, 1965), 15.

tradition that emphasizes community and tradition. They also appeal to practical knowledge (*phronēsis*) rather than simply theoretical knowledge.[72] To acknowledge the authority of people who know better than the individual is "not an abdication of reason, but . . . a *reasonable* judgement that the other is superior to oneself in judgement and insight."[73] Johnson and Victor L. Austin make the same point. Together with Alasdair MacIntyre and Gadamer, they oppose the tradition of the Enlightenment. Austin writes: "Authority is needed to counteract our built-in egoism, our preference for our own good over another's."[74]

Wisdom comes in many forms to address the complexities of situations in life. It has twelve forms of communication, including aphorisms, gnomic sayings, paradoxes, dialectic, similes and metaphors, and synonymous parallelism. The reason for this variety is the complexity and particularity of the issues in life that they address. Wisdom addresses the many-sidedness of life. In terms of skills it may apply to the capacity of women to spin cotton or wool (Exod. 35:25), work of goldsmiths (Jer. 10:9), skill of sailors (Ezek. 27:8), wisdom of administrators (Gen. 41:33, 39), managerial oversight over the tribes (Deut. 1:13, 15), or political advisers (Isa. 29:14; Jer. 18:18). In general terms it is shrewdness or cunning, or what today we might call being streetwise. It is an expanding capacity of mind, based on education and experience, rather than simple intellectual reflection. Proverbs traces increase in wisdom and stages in folly by using a number of words that cannot easily be translated into English. To use the usual English translations, the height of foolishness is often indicated by words such as "scoffer" or "scorner" (*lēṣ*); the "churlish man" (*nābāl*) may be less extreme; the "stupid person" (*'ĕwîl*) is merely "thick"; a person may simply be not too bright (*kĕsîl*); or finally someone may be "naïve" or "gullible" (*pĕtî*). On the positive side, wisdom is associated with moral qualities: for example, patience (Prov. 19:11), humility (29:23), self-control and discretion (18:21), peace and reconciliation (17:14), temperance or moderation (23:19-21), generosity (22:9), and hard work (6:6).

72. Gadamer, *Truth and Method*, 20, 277-85.

73. Ibid., 279 (emphasis original).

74. Victor Lee Austin, *Up with Authority: Why We Need Authority to Flourish as Human Beings* (London/New York: T&T Clark/Continuum, 2010), 15; cf. 16-39; and Alastair MacIntyre, *After Virtue: A Study in Moral Theory*, 2nd ed. (London: Duckworth, 1985), 62, 144, and passim.

In the New Testament many books expound qualities of wisdom. J. B. Mayor observed many years ago: "Wisdom is the principal thing to which James gives the same prominence as St Paul to faith, St. John to love, and St. Peter to hope."[75] Wisdom in James helps the Christian to overcome trials. James declares: "If any of you is lacking in wisdom, ask God, who gives to all generously and ungrudgingly, and it will be given you" (1:5 NRSV). Indeed James contains three clusters of biblical passages on the subject of wisdom: 1:5-8; 1:12-18; and 3:13-18. The third passage lists wisdom qualities needed most of all by leaders or teachers including "gentleness born of wisdom" (3:13), humility (3:14), self-discipline (3:16), and sincerity and integrity (3:17). Leslie Mitton presses the point: "James proceeds to insist that true wisdom and understanding are not to be identified with a merely intellectual cleverness. Their genuineness is proved by the quality of conduct which they produce."[76]

Jesus often used wisdom sayings. Sometimes these take the form of aphorisms, or pithy, memorable, short sentences. One example comes from the well-known Sermon on the Mount. For example, Jesus declares: "Blessed are you poor, for yours is the kingdom of God. Blessed are you that hunger now, for you shall be satisfied. Blessed are you that weep now, for you shall laugh" (Matt. 5:3-12). We need not take this to such an extreme as James M. Robinson, Paul Hoffmann, and John Kloppenborg, who regarded Jesus as little more than an ancient sage.[77] Far more judicious and moderate is Ben Witherington's *Jesus the Sage*. This recognizes the importance of wisdom sayings in Jesus, especially in the triple tradition. For example, Witherington cites: "The Sabbath was delivered to you, you were not delivered to the Sabbath."[78]

Wisdom sayings are not confined to Jesus and James. It is well known that the term "wisdom" featured at Corinth especially. There are about twenty-seven uses of "wise" and "wisdom" (Greek *sophos* and *sophia*) in 1 Corinthians, with only six in the other major epistles. Wisdom, therefore,

75. J. B. Mayor, *The Epistle of James* (London: Macmillan, 1897), 36.

76. C. Leslie Mitton, *The Epistle of James* (London: Marshall, Morgan & Scott, 1966), 134.

77. John S. Kloppenborg, *The Formation of Q Transcripts in Ancient Wisdom Collections* (Philadelphia: Fortress, 1987); and James M. Robinson, John S. Kloppenborg, and Paul Hoffmann (eds.), *The Critical Edition of Q* (Minneapolis: Fortress, 2000).

78. Ben Witherington, *Jesus the Sage: The Pilgrimage of Wisdom* (Minneapolis: Augsburg/Fortress, 2000), 155-208 at 167.

was a catchword in the Corinthian community. Hence Paul stresses that
the wisdom he seeks is the wisdom given *by God* and not merely human
wisdom. His critique of wisdom comes to a climax in 1 Corinthians 3:18:
"Do not deceive yourselves. If you think that you are wise . . . , you should
become fools so that you may become wise" (NRSV). This becomes one of
the reversals of the cross. Wisdom comes from God as a gift, although it is
still associated with moral character. Paul's main target is that of manipu-
lative rhetoric.[79] In Paul wisdom is closely associated with Christ and the
message of the cross, in contrast to self-reliant, arrogant, assertive wisdom.
This merely underlines the Old Testament tradition of wisdom as a gift of
God, which requires humility and teachability. Parallel with this thought is
Paul's interesting use of the word "to know," where the verb *ginōskō* is posi-
tive, in contrast to the noun *gnōsis*, which is negative, because it is in danger
of implying that knowledge is a *completed* possession, rather than a process.
In Colossians wisdom is also two-sided. The Colossians must not imagine
that claims about wisdom outclass claims for the all-sufficiency of Christ. At
all events, in Paul wisdom is closely associated with the revelation of God, a
theme that I shall take up in chapters 7–8.

I have noted that wisdom, especially in the Old Testament, is communal,
corporate, and related to past generations. There is a parallel for Christians
in the social dimension of the church. Even in other contexts, the lonely,
isolated individual is more vulnerable to doubt or skepticism than a person
embedded in the community. The example of Kierkegaard is a telling one.
No one can doubt his Christian faith; but, as I observed, he could at times
exclaim: "My doubt is terrible." He cut himself off from the Danish church,
and the results are all too apparent. No part of this chapter argues that all
doubt and skepticism is due to less than adequate moral virtues. Nor does
it argue that social context cannot be abused by imposing mere convention.
However, the points are worth noting in particular circumstances.

79. Cf. Stephen M. Pogoloff, *Logos and Sophia: The Rhetorical Situation of 1 Corinthians*,
Society of Biblical Literature Dissertation Series 134 (Atlanta: Scholars Press, 1992).

CHAPTER 3

Doubt and Belief

Doubt in the Old Testament

One very practical question about doubt is whether it is ever compatible with belief. Readers of the New Testament may recall the supplicant's words: "I believe; help my unbelief." Do we, in practice, allow that there can be degrees of belief? On the one hand, Erasmus wrote in his *The Praise of Folly* that "nothing can be clearly known"; yet James Atkinson regards him as "a sincere and enlightened believer in Christianity." Atkinson even insists: "Erasmus forwarded the Reformation . . . by reviving classical, biblical, and patristic studies."[1] Further, Locke implied that we could experience degrees of belief; Newman implied that we could not.

John Suk, author of *Not Sure: A Pastor's Journey from Faith to Doubt* (cited in chap. 1), remains a diligent pastor in the Christian Reformed Church. He reminds us that concepts of faith are important, because "some contemporary misconceptions about faith . . . have not helped me on my own journey."[2] He also quotes Lewis Smedes, an ethicist from Fuller Theological Seminary, as admitting: "Sometimes I hang on to my faith by my fingernails."[3] Doubt is compatible with faith, and we should not be ashamed

---

1. James Atkinson, *The Great Light: Luther and the Reformation* (Grand Rapids: Eerdmans/Exeter: Paternoster, 1968), 78.

2. John Suk, *Not Sure: A Pastor's Journey from Faith to Doubt* (Grand Rapids: Eerdmans, 2011), 7.

3. Ibid., 3.

of it. Suk directs us to Psalm 77, where the psalmist appears to entertain doubts: "Are his [God's] promises at an end for all time? Has God forgotten to be gracious? Has he in anger shut up his compassion? And I say, 'It is my grief that the right hand of the Most High has changed'" (77:8–10 NRSV).

Illness can bring many doubts, especially if medication includes hallucinogenic drugs with their side effects. Suk recollects: "I swayed back and forth between belief and disbelief."[4] On one side, he lost his appetite for the institutional church; on the other hand, he found the pluralism of postmodernism fractured and unsettling, with Christian individualists treating even the church as a consumer marketplace, seeking to find better preachers, better choirs, better youth groups, and so on.[5] Sometimes we are overwhelmed; but Suk, like many others, finds doubt a cleansing, if also painful, experience.

We should never forget the further role of depression, mental strain, and trauma in promoting doubt and even despair. In the Old Testament, 1 Kings 18:19–40 recounts the initial triumph of the prophet Elijah over the 450 prophets of the ba'ālîm, the local, pagan gods of land and agriculture, championed by Queen Jezebel. Elijah laid down the challenge of a contest on Mount Carmel: "You call on the name of your god and I will call on the name of the LORD; the god who answers by fire is indeed God" (18:24).[6] The prophets of Baal called on their nature god from morning until noon, crying, "O Baal, answer us!" But there was no answer (18:26). Elijah mocked them, as they jumped upon their altar: "Cry aloud! Surely he is a god; either he is meditating, or he has wandered away, . . . perhaps he is asleep" (18:27). They cried aloud, and cut themselves with stones, but there was no voice (18:28–29). Then Elijah repaired the altar of the Lord and soaked it with water three times and laid a sacrificial bull on the wood (18:30–34): "Then the fire of the LORD fell and consumed the burnt offering, the wood, the stones, and the dust, and even licked up the water" (18:38). Finally all the people fell on their faces and said: "The LORD indeed is God" (18:39). Yet a second providential act of God followed in the coming of rain in a time of drought and famine.

After such a resounding victory, however, not surprisingly, following

4. Ibid., 67.
5. Ibid., 114, 130.
6. All Bible quotations in this section from the NRSV.

such a peak of elation and high activity, Elijah suffered an exhaustive reaction and became deeply depressed and even doubting. This intensified when Jezebel threatened him with personal revenge. He was afraid and fled for his life (19:3). He fled into the wilderness, sat down under a tree, and asked that he might die: "It is enough, . . . LORD" (perhaps: "I have had enough"). He continued: "Take away my life, for I am no better than my ancestors" (19:4). In his exhaustion and weary depression, he fell asleep. Meanwhile he was strengthened by an angel who came to feed him.

Then the word of the Lord came, saying: "What are you doing here, Elijah?" Elijah reported what had occurred on Mount Carmel, but in despair he added, "I alone am left, and they are seeking my life" (19:10). This question and reply were repeated. Wind, fire, and earthquake followed, but as both Scripture and the well-known hymn "Dear Lord and Father of Mankind" recount: "The LORD was not in the wind . . . not in the earthquake . . . not in the fire," but in a quiet voice. The Lord commissioned him to return to anoint Hazael, Jehu, and Elisha to finish his work by military and prophetic means. The voice of God concluded: "I will leave seven thousand in Israel . . . that have not bowed to Baal" (19:18). Matters began to look different in a perspective that eclipsed the doubt and despair that had dominated Elijah during his time of intense depression. We see a believer who passed through a time of deep doubts.

Elijah is not the only character in the Bible who suffered doubt arising partly from depression. Several psalms witness to this situation, and the book of Job may be the most well known. The book opens with Job as a prosperous farmer who was "blameless and upright, one who feared God and turned away from evil" (1:1). The prologue to the book then portrays Satan as asking God: "Does Job fear God for nothing?" (1:9). He suggests that human righteousness and goodness occur only when all is well and people prosper. In order to dispel the myth, Job's piety is tested by a series of disasters. First his oxen and donkeys, then his sheep and servants, and finally his family are destroyed. At this stage Job simply responds: "The LORD gave, and the LORD has taken away; blessed be the name of the LORD" (1:21). But disasters intensify. Job becomes covered in debilitating sores, and most of his friends desert him. Job begins to become depressed. He asks: "Why is light given to one in misery, and life to the bitter in soul, who long for death, but it does not come?" (3:20-21). Job's doubts lead to frustration: "O that my vexation were weighed, and all my calamity laid in the balances!" (6:2). His depression increases. He cries: "I am allotted months of emptiness, and nights of misery are apportioned to me" (7:3). He adds (as many in the depths of despair have cried): "I loathe my life; I would not live forever" (7:16).

Job's three friends (popularly known as "Job's comforters") are of no help at all. As misery accumulates, Job gradually comes to terms with the question "can you find out the deep things of God?" (11:7). He *cannot* fathom the ways of God. Doubt increases. Job cries out: "If I go forward, he [God] is not there; or backward, I cannot perceive him" (23:8). Many further chapters trace the drama, until Job finally comes face to face with God. The epilogue comes in Job 42, although some debate its authorship and integrity with the rest of the Book, because it seems to "solve" the problem of suffering too easily, or perhaps not at all. In this chapter Job says: "Now my eye sees you" (42:5), and the Lord restores Job's fortunes. Nevertheless most of the book traces the despair of a man who *believes* in God; he is innocent, as far as he can perceive, but he cannot find God. In the end he acknowledges that God is beyond his understanding and that God is ultimately in control of human affairs. What is clear is, first, that human goodness does not depend on human prosperity and, second, that despair readily brings doubt, even if Job is eventually vindicated.

The Psalms presuppose a variety of situations, and sometimes we can only speculate about their historical backgrounds. Nevertheless, some are clearly psalms of lament and grief, such as: "My God. . . . Why have you forsaken me? Why are you so far from helping me, from the words of my groaning?" (22:1). This was later spoken in prayer by Jesus Christ during tortuous death on the cross. The psalm continues: "I am poured out like water . . . my heart is like wax" (22:14). The "preacher" in Ecclesiastes also cries: "I hated life, because what is done under the sun was grievous to me; for all is vanity and a chasing after wind" (2:17). The preacher is not always full of doubts and even cynical doubts, but this makes the point that belief and doubt may sometimes be less than coherent and consistent. All our examples represent believers who doubt, not least because of trying circumstances or depression. As we shall see, much depends on the context in life.

To return to Suk's *Not Sure*, in spite of all his biographical descriptions of doubt, Suk includes several passages that relate to the recovery of belief. For example, as well as rehearsing the promises of God, he compares the positive attitude of a couple on the verge of breaking up their marriage, who share together times of happiness in the past, from photograph albums and so on. In this light he cites the Psalms as often saying: "I will call to mind the deeds of the LORD; I will remember your wonders of old" (77:11).[7] Toward the end of his book, he reminds us that whatever we think, God is greater than our hearts.[8] This reminds me of how too often people say in testimonies: "*My faith* saved me," when they surely mean (or should mean) "*God* or *Christ* saved me."

Can we now provide a more philosophical and theological explanation of how faith and doubt can operate simultaneously? The dispositional account of belief enables us to see how doubt and belief may depend on different situations and given contexts in life. Wittgenstein promoted this view in outline, but H. H. Price expounds it in detail and informs much of the discussion below.

Belief as a Disposition

The traditional account of belief as an inner mental occurrence points us in an unhelpful direction by seeming to suggest that introspection provides a useful way of understanding belief. Price calls this "occurrence analysis." He writes: "The modern way of treating belief is quite different." When we say "he believes that . . ." we are making a dispositional statement that is "equivalent to a series of conditional statements describing what he would be likely to say or do or feel, if such and such circumstances were to arise."[9]

Price provides many examples that explain the point. Believers would assert (either mentally or aloud) their belief, if they heard someone else denying it or expressing doubt about it. If the belief were falsified, they would feel surprise and disappointment. If the belief had practical consequences, they would live on the assumption that it was true. Price comments: "Belief shows itself or manifests itself in *various* sorts of circumstances. . . . But it is not itself an occurrence."[10]

7. Ibid., 135.
8. Ibid., 207.
9. H. H. Price, *Belief* (London: Allen & Unwin/New York: Humanities Press, 1969), 19–24 at 20.
10. Ibid., 20 (emphasis added).

On this view, Price continues: "It makes no sense to say of someone at 4.30 p.m., 'He is now believing that it is going to rain.'"[11] A better example might be to ask: "Does a believer cease to believe (or become an unbeliever) when he or she falls asleep?" In his *Zettel*, Wittgenstein observes that "an interrupted version of belief would not be a period of unbelief . . . e.g. [when he falls into] sleep. "[12]

Both Price and Wittgenstein explore the *performative* character of expressing belief. Wittgenstein begins: "Believing . . . is a kind of disposition of the believing person. This is shown to me in the case of someone else by his behaviour, and by his words."[13] He declares: "If there were a verb meaning 'to believe falsely,' it would not have any significant first person present indicative."[14] He adds: "My own relation to my words is wholly different from other people's."[15] In Price's words, belief is sometimes like "taking a stand," or at least "inviting our hearers to accept what we believe . . . 'I believe' has this taking-a-stand-character. . . . It also, as it were, offers a guarantee . . . 'I believe that p,' considered as a piece of social intercourse, does have this performatory aspect."[16]

Dallas M. High also supports the speech act or performative character of "I believe," especially in the light of Wittgenstein and Austin. Many uses of "I believe," he says, "are direct performances of action, like 'promising.' [They] must be distinguished from *reports of* action."[17] Such uses do not report a psychological event. He declares: "First-person performances are the requisite" of such language, and these require "personal backing."[18] In this vein, Price regards differences of degree in belief as not so much differences of certainty and doubt about what is believed, but as degrees of guarantee or personal backing concerning such belief.

Richard S. Briggs, Dietmar Neufeld, Colin Brown, and Daniel Strett

11. Ibid., 20–21.

12. Ludwig Wittgenstein, *Zettel* (Oxford: Blackwell, 1967), §85.

13. Ludwig Wittgenstein, *Philosophical Investigations*, 2nd ed. (Oxford: Blackwell, 1958), 191–92.

14. Ibid., 190.

15. Ibid., 192.

16. Price, *Belief*, 30, 31, 32.

17. Dallas M. High, *Language, Persons, and Belief* (New York: Oxford University Press, 1967), 155 (emphasis added).

18. Ibid., 158–59.

consider the explicit dimension of a speech act in an expression of confession.[19] Briggs begins with the confession "Jesus is Lord" (1 Cor. 12:1–3); Neufeld examines confession and denial in 1 John 2:22–23, 26; 4:1–4; and other passages "from the perspective of . . . Austin's speech act theory."[20] Briggs declares: "Confession has often . . . taken the form of reciting a 'creed' or more generally a song or hymn, as an address to God or Christ."[21] He then refers to Vernon Neufeld's *Earliest Christian Confessions* (1963) and to Oscar Cullmann's book of the same title (1940), concluding, with Neufeld, that "the confession of Jesus as the Christ was in the first instance a personal confession of faith."[22] Cullmann sees the confessions as merging with early creeds.[23]

Many writers speculate about the circumstances that called for personal backing for belief in early Christian confessions. They most likely include Christian baptism, the courtroom (1 Tim. 6:12), persecution, the imperial cult (as Cullmann and many others suggest), martyrdom, and so on. Essentially, confessions offer personal backing for a belief and are hardly less "speech acts" than promising. Austin would probably call such confessions "commissives," for they are self-involving, committing the speaker to take a stand and to accept the consequences. Hugh Williamson suggests a wide variety of contexts in which confessions emerged, but all are polemical, as a response to rival claims to lordship, whether that of Caesar or of idols (1 Cor. 12:2), or whatever threatens to dominate the believer's life.[24] Neufeld regards confessions in 1 John as involving taking a stand on christological orthodoxy, especially against docetism.[25] But David Peterson regards them above all

19. Richard S. Briggs, *Words in Action: Speech-Act Theory and Biblical Interpretation* (Edinburgh: T&T Clark, 2001), 183–216; Dietmar Neufeld, *Re-conceiving Texts as Speech-Acts: An Analysis of 1 John*, Biblical Interpretation Monograph 7 (Leiden: Brill, 1994); Colin Brown, "The Hermeneutics of Confession and Accusation," *Canadian Theological Journal* 30 (1995): 460–71; and Daniel Strett, *They Went Out from Us: The Opponents in 1 John* (Berlin: de Gruyter, 2011), 195–217.

20. Neufeld, *Re-conceiving Texts as Speech-Acts*, 3, 82–132.

21. Briggs, *Words in Action*, 188.

22. Ibid., 193; cf. Vernon H. Neufeld, *The Earliest Christian Confessions* (Leiden: Brill, 1963); and Oscar Cullmann, *The Earliest Christian Confessions* (London: Lutterworth, 1949).

23. Cullmann, *Earliest Christian Confessions*, 11.

24. Hugh Williamson, *Jesus Is Lord: A Personal Rediscovery* (Nottingham: Crossway, 1993).

25. Neufeld, *Re-conceiving Texts as Speech-Acts*, 119.

as acts of worship.[26] Cullmann and Briggs also view Philippians 2:6–11 primarily as a confessional formula in the context of worship.[27] Others stress the ethical context of humility, like that of Christ.

Most people agree that the various parts of Christian worship are best described as *acts*: acts of confession, acts of thanksgiving, acts of adoration, and so on. Those who worship are not merely describing or reporting their emotions; they are *doing* things in which they are deeply involved. In other words, they are what Austin calls "performatives."

All this adds force to the claim that the active belief and its outward expression constitute a disposition to speak and act in appropriate circumstances. We do not spontaneously recite the creed aloud in an underground train or voluntarily enact a formal expression of belief when it is not implicitly challenged.

Can Doubt and Faith Be Compatible?

Our second question was: does doubt always signify unbelief? I have already cited the cry of the father of the demon-possessed boy, "Lord, I believe, help my unbelief" (Mark 9:24 NRSV). I may also cite the strange and paradoxical cases of Jonah and, perhaps also in early modern times, Kierkegaard.

Price has wonderful examples of what he calls "half-belief," of which Jonah and Kierkegaard would be prime candidates. Their intensity of conviction is not halfhearted, but strong and passionate. The problem in Price's words is that on some occasions we act, feel, and think in the same way as a believer; but on other occasions we act, feel, and think like unbelievers or doubters.[28] The book of Jonah is a satire on half-belief and is full of irony and paradox. In Jonah 1 we see the prophet taking ship to Tarshish to flee "from the presence of the LORD" (1:3), as if he did not believe in the omnipresence of the one God. His flight was because God had commanded him to preach to the inhabitants of pagan Nineveh (1:1–2), and Jonah did not wish to preach

26. David Peterson, *Engaging with God: A Biblical Theology of Worship* (Leicester: Apollos, 1992).

27. Briggs, *Words in Action*, 200; and Cullmann, *Earliest Christian Confessions*, 22–23.

28. Price, *Belief*, 302–14 at 305. Cf. also E. M. Good, *Irony in the Old Testament* (London: SPCK, 1965), 39–55.

to pagans. When a storm threatens to break up the ship, all pray to their gods, except Jonah (1:4–6)! The sailors cast lots to see who has caused calamity to the ship, and the lot falls upon Jonah (1:7–8).

When the sailors question Jonah, it is, he thinks, the time to rehearse the testimony of a believer. He declares: "I am a Hebrew . . . I worship the LORD, the God of heaven, who made the sea and the dry land" (1:9). Here is Jonah, the orthodox believer! Jonah continues his believing confession: "I know it is because of me that this great storm has come upon you." So they pick Jonah up and throw him into the sea (1:12–15). As a believer he goes to his death. Now, at the end of Jonah 1, in what E. M. Good calls a blend "of the miraculous and the ludicrous,"[29] God prepares and provides "a large fish to swallow up Jonah; and Jonah was in the belly of the fish three days and three nights" (1:17).

The whole of Jonah 2 recounts Jonah's prayer as a believer. Whether Jonah deliberately echoed the poetic style of the Psalms, or whether the narrator ironically assimilated Jonah's words to the style of a devout psalmist, the prophet says all the "right orthodox things" for a serious believer to pray. Not only does he pray "I called to the LORD out of my distress" (2:2); but he also laments "how shall I look again upon your holy temple?" (2:4). He dramatizes how "the waters closed in over me; . . . weeds were wrapped around my head. . . . As my life was ebbing away, I remembered the LORD. . . . Deliverance belongs to the LORD!" (2:5–9). Good suggests that the ironic character of the passage reaches a climax in the words "the fish . . . spewed Jonah out upon the dry land," that is, it literally spat him out as unpalatable![30]

The paradox, or clash of believing and unbelieving worlds, continues. In 3:1–4 Jonah is glad to be commissioned to proclaim judgment and disaster upon Nineveh. It is possible that the dimension of "three days' walk across it" (the city) could be part of a deliberate hyperbole, to stress the irony or satire. But to Jonah's dismay "the people of Nineveh believed God; . . . everyone . . . put on sackcloth" (3:5). Even the king of Nineveh put on sackcloth "and sat in ashes" (3:6). He called a fast and commanded that the people "cry mightily to God. All shall turn from their evil ways. . . . Who knows? God may relent" (3:8–9). In fact God did this (3:10). The punch line comes at the beginning

29. Good, *Irony in the Old Testament*, 46.
30. Ibid., 45.

of Jonah 4: "But this was very displeasing to Jonah, and he became angry" (4:1). He explains to God, "That is why I fled to Tarshish . . . ; for I knew that you are a gracious God and merciful, slow to anger" (4:2). He has let the cat out of the bag!

In 4:5 Jonah left the city to sulk over his disappointment. He made a booth to give shelter for himself. In 4:6 "God appointed a bush," perhaps an ironic but true comment on the need to improve his protection from the sun. Then (surely with yet more satire or irony), "God appointed a worm that attacked the bush" (4:7). When the bush withered, Jonah basked in his anger: "It is better for me to die than live" (4:8). We may compare this outburst with his pious prayer for deliverance from death in Jonah 2.

The ultimate climax of the book comes in 4:10–11. God addresses him: "You are concerned about the bush! . . . Should not I be concerned about Nineveh, that great city, in which there are more than a hundred and twenty thousand persons . . . and also many animals?" (4:11). Compare the two worlds. Jonah occupies a petty self-centered world of vindictiveness, exclusivism, and national self-interest. God's world embraces generosity, grace, and compassion. In Price's terms, Jonah displays "half-belief." It would be impossible to claim that Jonah never truly believes. Nevertheless this remains within his self-centered horizons of half-belief, which leads to doubt simultaneously with moments of genuine belief.

Our second example is somewhat more complex. In Kierkegaard, similarly, we often see two competing worlds or two contexts. On one side he defines faith as "staking one's life" or "being sharpened into an 'I.'"[31] Personal decision, commitment, and obedience are required. Yet partly on the basis of Abraham's facing the imminent sacrifice of Isaac, faith becomes a self-contradiction. God had shown him that all nations were to be blessed through Isaac. Yet now he is commanded "to slay the son of promise."[32] This is seemingly to surrender all hope of the promises, and the decision of faith seems to override the ethical.

The world of faith is not one of intellectual assent to propositions for

---

31. Søren Kierkegaard, *Concluding Unscientific Postscript* (Princeton: Princeton University Press, 1941), 51; and idem, *The Journals of Søren Kierkegaard* (Oxford: Oxford University Press, 1938), 533.

32. Søren Kierkegaard, *Fear and Trembling* and *The Sickness unto Death* (Princeton: Princeton University Press, 1941), 77.

Kierkegaard; it issues in obedience and worship, not intellectual argument. Kierkegaard declares: "To prove the existence of one who is present is the most shameless affront, since it is an attempt to make him ridiculous. . . . One proves God's existence by worship . . . not by proofs."[33] Orthodox Christianity is too often a way of "talking about" God, he says, instead of "being a Christian."[34] Faith, he declares, is "believing against the understanding."[35] Faith is always accompanied by doubt, not least because it has to be sustained moment by moment. Perhaps because he cut himself off from the church and regarded faith as "individual," at one minute he can write in his *Journal* of his confidence in "the objective reality of Christ's atonement";[36] but he can write in the very same year (1838): "My doubt is terrible. Nothing can withstand it. It is a cursed hunger."[37] On 24 April 1838, he writes: "My self-isolation cannot be broken. . . . An immediate certainty about my relation to Christ I cannot acquire."[38] Yet he also writes, within his other world of belief: "The whole of my work as an author is related . . . to the problem of 'becoming a Christian.'"[39]

It would fly against most of the evidence to claim, therefore, that Kierkegaard was not a sincere Christian believer. Yet it would also fly against the evidence to claim that he never experienced doubt, or that doubt and faith were incompatible. Indeed if Kierkegaard is right to regard faith as being renewed moment by moment, doubt must regularly arise to be conquered by renewed acts of will to believe. Admittedly faith is not always or simply a matter of will, as we shall see in chapter 5, but often it may seem so.

Doubt as Questioning

Nevertheless, R. G. Collingwood and Hans-Georg Gadamer are not the only thinkers to study and expound the logic of questions and their role in discov-

33. Kierkegaard, *Concluding Unscientific Postscript*, 485.

34. Søren Kierkegaard, *Attack on "Christendom"* (Oxford: Oxford University Press, 1946), 150; and idem, *The Last Years: Journals, 1853–55* (London: Collins, 1965), 336.

35. Kierkegaard, *Last Years*, 336.

36. Kierkegaard, *Journals*, 59–63.

37. Ibid., 89.

38. Ibid., 242–43.

39. Søren Kierkegaard, *The Point of View for My Work as an Author* (Oxford: Oxford University Press, 1939/New York: Harper, 1962), 5–6.

ery. In one sense, this tradition goes back to Socrates (469–399 BC). Socrates believed that he had a mission to expose false claims to wisdom, which were often merely expressions of ignorance or opinion parading in the guise of knowledge. Therefore he developed the technique of asking awkward questions, especially about the foundations of knowledge, meanings, ethics, and politics. These were often useful in exposing the dubious rhetoric of the Sophists. Allegedly on the lips of Socrates, Plato often made such questions very complex. This occurs notably in the *Republic*, where these questions led to exposing the difference between belief or opinion (Greek *doxa*) and knowledge (*epistēmē*). Today the method may often be used in pedagogy. A teacher, for example, may often ask: "Why do you say that?" "Is this always the case?" "What would be the counterargument to this?" Such questions aim to explore the student's thinking more deeply.

It is a truism that doubt and questioning play an integral part of scientific method. Every scientific theory first faces the question: "What is the evidence for this?" "What would be the outcome of that?" (I will explore this further when examining Kuhn, Popper, and Lakatos.) Belnap and Steel in *The Logic of Questions and Answers* raise not only philosophical and semantic issues, but also enter the field of computer programming and artificial intelligence.[40]

It should not surprise us that a linguistic philosopher, F. Waismann, writes on the subject "Towards a Logic of Questions."[41] He declares: "The question is the first groping step of the mind in its journeying that leads towards new horizons. The great mind is the great questioner. . . . To sense riddles and problems where others see the flat road of convention . . . constitutes the philosophical spirit. *Questions lead us on and over the barriers of traditional opinions.*"[42]

Waismann concedes that questions may also seduce us and lead us astray. Hence thinking about the nature and propriety of questions is vital. Questions, he says, incite us to search. Questions and requests constitute a sort of lever, which may set hidden questions or requests in motion. A

40. N. D. Belnap and Thomas B. Steel, *The Logic of Questions and Answers* (New Haven: Yale University Press, 1976).

41. F. Waismann, *The Principles of Linguistic Philosophy* (London: Macmillan/New York: Saint Martin's Press, 1965), 387–418.

42. Ibid., 405 (emphasis added).

proposition is likely to close possibilities, to bring them to an end, as if to suggest that everything has been settled. Questions not only leave matters open, but provoke discovery. Waismann concludes: "We can . . . extend the field of vision of the questioner, loosen his prejudices, and guide his gaze in different directions," if he consents.[43]

Earlier than Waismann the importance of the logic of question and answer was explored by Robin G. Collingwood (1889–1943). Collingwood was born in Lancashire, England, and was Waynflete Professor of Metaphysical Philosophy at Oxford from 1935 until 1941. He is nowadays perhaps best known through his book *The Idea of History* and through Gadamer's allusion to his logic of questions and answers in his *Truth and Method*.[44] Gadamer recognizes his influence on hermeneutics and his stand against positivism and the imperialism of the methods of the natural sciences. Nevertheless Collingwood is seldom mentioned by name in major books on hermeneutics by Richard Palmer, Brice Wachterhauser, Gerald Bruns, and Kurt Muellner-Vollmer. Yet much of Collingwood's inspiration came from Wilhelm Dilthey, Schleiermacher's successor in hermeneutics, whom he called that "lonely and neglected genius."[45]

Like Gadamer, Collingwood opposed positivism and the extension and imposition of scientific method onto the humanities and social sciences. Dilthey was concerned not only with texts, but also with human life and social institutions. One of his themes was the historian's "reliving" (German *nacherleben*) the life (*Leben*) of what was to be understood. Similarly, Collingwood comments: "The historian who relives the past in his own mind" enlarges his understanding.[46] His one reservation about Dilthey, as in Gadamer, was his over-attention to psychology. But all three thinkers argued that the past was not simply a dead past merely to be described in positivist or empiricist terms. In his *Essay on Metaphysics* he declares: "Every statement that anybody ever makes is made in answer to a [an implied?] question."[47] In terms of under-

---

43. Ibid., 417.

44. Hans-Georg Gadamer, *Truth and Method*, 2nd ed. (London: Sheed & Ward, 1989), 371–79, 513–16.

45. Robin G. Collingwood, *The Idea of History* (Oxford/New York: Oxford University Press, 1946), 171.

46. Ibid., 173.

47. Robin Collingwood, *Essay in Metaphysics* (Oxford/New York: Oxford University Press, 1940), 23.

standing (hermeneutics) any question about the truth of what is presupposed is irrelevant. Like Gadamer, Collingwood prefers questions to problems in the understanding and discovery of truth.

Before turning to Gadamer, I note how one educationalist discovers huge practical consequences of Collingwood's approach for education. David Aldridge argues that this shows the superiority of ongoing dialogue of question and answer for students or pupils, rather than following some pre-formulated fixed syllabus of predetermined goals and outcomes worked out in advance and imposed on the teacher and student.[48] After many years of university teaching, I am inclined to agree, although the vocational importance of the syllabus must also be borne in mind.

Gadamer similarly compares free-floating problems with "questions that arise, and that derive their sense from their motivation."[49] Problems are usually or often abstractions, which may distract us from the temporal and social givenness of their contexts. Similarly Gadamer writes: "Reflection on the hermeneutical experience transforms problems back to questions that arise and that derive their sense from their motivation."[50] He declares: "The concept of the problem is clearly an abstraction, namely the detachment of the context of the question from the question that in fact first reveals it. . . . Such a problem has fallen out of the motivated context of questioning, from which it receives the clarity of its sense."[51] Problems, he claims, presuppose a point outside history. Like Collingwood, Gadamer insists that the historian, on the basis of hermeneutics, must "always . . . go beyond mere reconstruction."[52] He acknowledges the work of Collingwood as a pioneer of this subject. I do not believe that this genuinely undermines Pannenberg's insistence on the importance of statement, certainly at a later stage of understanding.

Any implication of doubt involved in questioning—whether in Socrates, contemporary scientific methods, Waismann, Collingwood, or Gadamer—should be distinguished sharply from methodological doubt in Descartes. These thinkers did not promote universal doubt or pseudocertainty. In a

48. David Aldridge, "The Logical Priority of the Question," *Journal of Philosophy of Education* 47 (2013): 71–85.

49. Gadamer, *Truth and Method*, 369–79 at 377.

50. Ibid., 377.

51. Ibid., 376.

52. Ibid., 374.

masterly way, Bernard Lonergan dissociates the "naïve realism" of much classic science from contemporary scientific concerns with probability, and he emphatically distances the latter from Descartes.[53] Indeed on the subject of questions, he declares: "Context is a nest of interlocked or interwoven questions and answers. . . . When there are no further relevant questions, there are no further insights to complement, correct, or qualify, those that had been reached."[54] ⁄

One way of comparing classic scientific method with those of contemporary sciences is to compare the contemporary research methods discussed by Kuhn, Popper, and Lakatos with earlier classic Newtonian projects. This can be seen, for example, especially in their common work *Criticism and the Growth of Knowledge*.[55] Thomas S. Kuhn (1922–96) in his introductory essay attacked Karl Popper (1902–94) for his emphasis on falsification or for "the tradition of claims, counterclaims, and debates over fundamentals, which . . . have characterised philosophy and much of social science ever since."[56] This, Kuhn says, does not allow for "moments of crisis," when a group opinion may change. Within the new group's opinion, criteria of evidence change in the new context. He cites the example of the change of shared theory from astrology to astronomy: "On some occasions, at least, tests are not requisite to the relations through which science advances."[57] This plays a fundamental role in Kuhn's *The Structure of Scientific Revolutions*, in which his well-known notion of paradigm plays a major part.[58] In due course Lakatos criticizes Kuhn for using "a conceptual framework . . . [that] is *socio-psychological*."[59] There seems to be much truth in this critique, and paradigms have become,

---

53. Bernard Lonergan, *Insight: A Study in Human Understanding* (New York: Harper & Row, 1978 [orig. 1957]), 408–11; idem, *Method in Theology* (London: Darton, Longman & Todd, 1972), 315–17.

54. Lonergan, *Method in Theology*, 163–64.

55. Imre Lakatos and Alan Musgrave (eds.), *Criticism and the Growth of Knowledge* (Cambridge: Cambridge University Press, 1970).

56. T. S. Kuhn, "The Logic of Discovery," in *Criticism and the Growth of Knowledge*, ed. Imre Lakatos and Alan Musgrave (Cambridge: Cambridge University Press, 1970), 1–23 at 6.

57. Ibid., 10.

58. T. S. Kuhn, *The Structure of Scientific Revolutions*, 2nd ed. (Chicago: University of Chicago Press, 1970).

59. Kuhn, "Reflections on My Critics," in *Criticism and the Growth of Knowledge*, ed. Imre Lakatos and Alan Musgrave (Cambridge: Cambridge University Press, 1970), 237 (emphasis added).

especially in theology, too much dependent on some supposed fashionable human consensus.

Imre Lakatos (1922–74) claims to move beyond the well-worn Kuhn-Popper debate. He traces the crude, popular misunderstanding of the supposed eclipse of the Newtonian paradigms by the Einsteinian one, as if the former had to be "replaced" by the latter.[60] Kuhn, he suggests, draws too much inspiration from this example. Many remain convinced that a "hard fact approach" may serve to disprove a universal theory.[61]

At first sight Lakatos seems to be more than sympathetic with Popper's approach, and they certainly do overlap. In Popper's view the attempt to test an accumulated experience by a criterion of falsification tested the conjectured hypotheses of predecessors in order to arrive at truth through this process of "critical rationalism." The method consciously built on the Socratic method of questioning. Invalid competing theories would be filtered out, as knowledge might be from opinion. Kuhn approaches the problem more historically and sociologically. When a paradigm, or generally agreed consensus view, becomes historically overtaken, the old and new paradigms become "incommensurable," that is, they allegedly share no common criterion of truth that fits both. Lakatos agreed with Popper that counterexamples could play an important role, not least in mathematics. But he replaced his emphasis on theory by a broader and longer program that he called "a research programme." He agreed with Kuhn that indeed historical progress played a vital role, but also criticized him for downplaying rationality, as against a merely sociological consensus of the day. This claim would amount to near pragmatism.

Lakatos, like Lonergan, emphasizes degrees of probability, especially when theories are unprovable or indemonstrable.[62] Concerning Popper's theory, he famously declares: "Science cannot *prove* any theory. But although science cannot prove, it can *disprove*, it can perform . . . repudiation of what is false."[63] He cites how Newton's theory (in one sense) replaced that of Des-

60. Lakatos, "Methodology of Scientific Research Programs," in *Criticism and the Growth of Knowledge*, ed. Imre Lakatos and Alan Musgrave (Cambridge: Cambridge University Press, 1970), 91–196 at 92.

61. Ibid., 94.

62. Ibid., 95.

63. Ibid.

cartes, and Einstein's that of Newton. But he effectively makes two assumptions about Popper, both concerning the observation of empirical data: "No factual proposition can ever be proved from an experiment. Propositions . . . cannot be derived from facts."[64]

This is because Lakatos shares Gadamer's view of facts. Gadamer considers the example of statistics here and declares: "What is established by statistics seems to be the language of facts, but which assertions these facts answer, and which facts would begin to speak if other questions were asked *are hermeneutical questions. Only a hermeneutical inquiry would legitimate the meaning of those facts, and thus the consequences that follow from them.*"[65] This constitutes one reason why I suspect virtually all questionnaires. The compiler or computer programmer of questionnaires is too often manipulating what counts as facts or outcomes. Similarly, Lakatos has little confidence in evaluating one theory at a time against its competitors. Discovery, he writes, "involves a *succession* of theories, not one theory. . . . Such series of theories are usually connected by a remarkable continuity that welds them *into research programmes.*"[66]

These research programs are heuristic; that is, they help us discover or learn something for ourselves. Lakatos distinguishes "negative heuristic," which warns us of probable falsification; and "positive heuristic," which indicates what paths we can best pursue.[67] Lakatos's warnings against the over-narrowness of both Kuhn and Popper also warn us not to expect too much from the over-easy use of paradigms, incommensurability, and falsification in theology, even if these may retain some degree of usefulness. What he also shows is the extreme complexity of questions, doubts, and beliefs, especially in the sciences. Metaphors from the philosophy of science should not too easily be transferred to theology without careful reflection about their accuracy in a different field.

Collingwood, Waismann, Gadamer, Kuhn, and Lakatos do not provide easy reading. Is there nothing less technical and philosophical, which makes

64. Ibid., 99.
65. Hans-Georg Gadamer, "The Universality of the Hermeneutical Problem," in his *Philosophical Hermeneutics* (Berkeley: University of California Press, 1976), 11 (emphasis added); cf. pp. 3–17.
66. Lakatos, "Methodology of Scientific Research Programs," 132.
67. Ibid., 138–73.

the point concerning the creativity of doubt? I have established that not every kind of doubt in every situation is necessarily creative. But Robert Davidson provides one positive view of doubt, which is written "for the minister and the ordinary man and woman."[68] Davidson points out how often questioning arises in the Psalms, regards faith as part of pilgrimage, and traces this motif through the whole Old Testament. The argument is biblical rather than philosophical.

Can There Be Degrees of Doubt or Belief?

This question seems to raise the issue of a head-on collision between the opposite views of John Locke and John Henry Newman. Locke, like Descartes and Wittgenstein, is one of those philosophers who cannot be ignored if we are discussing doubt, faith, and certainty. His famous *Essay concerning Human Understanding* (1690) discusses mind, reason, and empiricism, as we have seen. Empiricists, especially Locke, George Berkeley (1685–1753), and David Hume (1711–76), held that all our knowledge is based on experience. Experience may include perception and reflection, but unlike Descartes, not "innate ideas." Images and knowledge come through the physical sciences to the mind from outside the mind, to form ideas. Hence, empiricists are usually also idealists. Simple ideas are those that proceed from "primary qualities," such as extension, motion, and solidity. Those ideas that come from "secondary qualities," such as color, taste, and smell, invite greater interpretive capacity on the part of the mind. More recently Nicholas Wolterstorff and other philosophers have turned their attention to Locke's hitherto neglected book 4, which discusses belief, reason, and the relation between faith and reason, as well as Locke's famous attack in chapter 19 on "subjective certainty" or "enthusiasm."[69] Wolterstorff also sees in book 4 a deeper and more subtle version of "foundationalism" than that of Descartes, that is, a system of justified or entitled belief. Thus Wolterstorff observes: "Locke's

---

68. Robert Davidson, *The Courage to Doubt* (London: SCM/Philadelphia: Trinity, 1983); quotation is from the *Expository Times* review printed on the cover.

69. Nicolas Wolterstorff, *John Locke and the Ethics of Belief* (Cambridge: Cambridge University Press, 1996).

main aim in Book 4 was to offer a theory of entitled [i.e., permitted, responsible] belief."[70]

For our purposes, the most fruitful chapters are chapter 15 on probability, chapter 16 on degrees of assent, and chapter 19 on enthusiasm. First, Locke rejects the notion of finding "certain truth."[71] Probability, he says, is "likeliness to be true."[72] Probability depends, first, on conformity with our own experience and, second, on the testimony of others. But the frequency and certainty of our two categories of observation make something "more or less probable."[73] In the chapter entitled "Degrees of Assent," Locke declares: "Our assent ought to be regulated by the grounds of probability . . . whereby its several degrees are, or ought to be, regulated."[74] Fallible memory, he urges, may reduce the degree of the probability and assent. Sometimes even error or mistakes may occur.[75]

Locke sets out a whole range of degrees of belief that, in turn, rest on degrees of probability that relate to the grounds for belief. Sometimes we imagine that belief is self-evident, when it is not so. At other times "our experience" may "produce confidence," which is enhanced by the "agreement of all others that mention it."[76] Yet testimony may become less convincing. For example: "The further removed [from historical events or reality, or equally from us], the less the proof becomes."[77]

It may seem as if Locke entirely links belief with rational probability, which may be the chief reason why Newman opposes it. But in fact Locke concludes: "The base testimony of divine revelation is the highest certainty," for God "cannot deceive or be deceived. . . . This carries with it an assurance beyond doubt. . . . Faith is a settled and sure principle of assent and assurance."[78] Locke was a Christian believer, and he wrote a commentary on the epistles of Paul.[79]

70. Ibid., xv.
71. Locke, *Essay*, 4.15.2.
72. Ibid., 4.15.3.
73. Ibid., 4.15.6.
74. Ibid., 4.16.1.
75. Ibid., 4.16.3.
76. Ibid., 4.16.7.
77. Ibid., 4.16.10.
78. Ibid., 4.16.14.
79. John Locke, *A Paraphrase and Notes on the Epistles of Paul to the Galatians, 1 and 2 Corinthians, Romans, and Ephesians* (London: Black Swan, 1707).

Yet he also expressed extreme caution about glib or over-easy appeals to reve-lation. His chapter 19, "Of Enthusiasm," is a blistering condemnation of those who "love not truth for truth's sake" but make appeals "beyond the degrees of that evidence."[80]

In this chapter, which at the time meant the kind of spirituality associ-ated with the Montanists, left-wing or magical reformers, and the earliest Quakers, Locke soundly condemns "a forwardness to dictate another's be-liefs" and "enthusiasm in which reason is taken away."[81] What Locke most critically attacks is an appeal to "immediate revelation . . . an opinion of a greater familiarity with God . . . [and] frequent communications from the Divine Spirit."[82] He declares: "Enthusiasm accepts its supposed illumina-tion without search and proof. . . . They [Enthusiasts] feel the hand of God moving them within, and the impulses of the Spirit, and [claim that they] cannot be mistaken in what they feel."[83] He adds: "The supposed internal light" must be examined soberly, to ask whether it is truly a revelation from God."[84] (This last probably refers to the early Quakers.) He ends by casting his net more widely, making some of his objections more understandable: "Revelation must be judged by reason. . . . I am far from denying that God can, or does, sometimes enlighten man's minds in the apprehending of certain truths . . . by the immediate assistance of the Holy Spirit. . . . But in such cases, too, we have reason and Scripture. . . . To know whether it be from God or no."[85]

We should not forget Locke's long seventeenth chapter on reason. He admits here that reason has "various significations," but he uses it to denote that capacity in humans that distinguishes them from animals. Reason is clearly a gift from God for "the discovery and finding out of truths" and for "making a right conclusion."[86] To sum up Locke's point, it is a high degree of belief that becomes "entitled belief."

John Henry Newman, however, in his *Grammar of Assent*, writes of

80. Locke, *Essay*, 4.19.1.
81. Ibid., 4.19.2–3.
82. Ibid., 4.19.5.
83. Ibid., 4.19.8.
84. Ibid., 4.19.10.
85. Ibid., 4.19.14, 16.
86. Ibid., 4.17.1, 3.

assent as "considered or unconditional" and concedes that his respect for
John Locke was so high that he admits: "I feel no pleasure in considering him
in the light of an opponent to abuse which I myself have ever cherished as
true."[87] He first argues that Locke had been inconsistent. For example, Locke
admitted that some propositions "border so near upon certainty that we
make no doubt at all about them."[88] Second, Newman distinguishes assent
from inference, which, he says, is always conditional. Newman resists any
notion that one could argue a person into faith. Chadwick aptly summarizes
Newman's position, "The faith of the simple is as certain as the faith of the
educated."[89]

Owen Chadwick sums up Newman's main point: "We cannot wait for
a long chain of arguments before we act. . . . Certainty is based only on
trust. . . . Some truth is certain, although to the philosopher only *proba-
ble*. . . . Newman was an intellectual who distrusted the intellect."[90] Newman
therefore coins the term "illative sense" to describe an act of assent that is
based, not on a long succession of a chain of arguments, but upon a body of
grounds in their totality. The word "illative" comes from Latin *illatus*, which
means "brought in" or "carried into," so it can refer to the gathering up of the
fragments of experience (e.g., the beauty of nature, pangs of conscience, the
experience of forgiveness) "into a single unified judgement, keeping together
tiny indications which produce certitude."

Newman writes: "Certitude is a mental state; certainty is a quality of
propositions. . . . Experience leads a syllogism only to probabilities."[91] He
continues: "The sole and final judgement on the validity of the accuracy of
an inference . . . committed to personal action . . . I have called the *Illative
Sense*, the use of the word 'sense' parallel to our use of it in 'good sense,'
'commonsense,' 'a sense of beauty.'"[92] K. C. Flynn appeals to Stanley Cavell's
argument that just as Wittgenstein was essentially offering a defense against

87. John H. Newman, *The Grammar of Assent* (New York: Doubleday, 1955), 138 = (Lon-
don: Longmans, 1947 [orig. 1870]), 122.
88. Ibid. (Doubleday), 139; (Longmans), 421–24; and Locke, *Essay*, 4.15.2.
89. Owen Chadwick, *Newman* (Oxford: Oxford University Press, 1983), 34.
90. Ibid., 35, 37.
91. Newman, *Grammar of Assent*, 345.
92. Ibid. (Doubleday), 270–99 at 270; (Longmans), 347–71 at 346; and Aidan Nichols,
"John Henry Newman and the Illative Sense: A Reconsideration," *Scottish Journal of Theology*
38 (1985): 347–68. Nichols stresses the part played by the voice of conscience.

skepticism, this was also Newman's overall aim.[93] Like Wittgenstein, New-
man appeals to the ordering of life, in his crowning achievement of formu-
lating the illative sense. Also like Wittgenstein, the illative sense in Newman
concerns the gathering up of numerous judgments of propositions, just as
certainty in Wittgenstein seems to be based on "a nest of propositions" or
a system of belief.

It is tempting to conclude that Locke and Newman are both correct
within their respective domains of argument, context, and comment. Their
frames of reference are different. Wolterstorff argues that many of Locke's
predecessors agreed about degrees of certainty and degrees of probability,
in wide-ranging discussions about certainty that had been taking place in
England. In these discussions, Wolterstorff argues: "The participants . . . were
themselves not entirely clear on the matter."[94] On the other hand, Newman
is largely speaking of trust and revelation and insisting that in this respect
probability is irrelevant to belief. In fact today committed Christians may
have different views about the role of probability. For example, Pannenberg
insists on the importance and role of argument in arriving at, and defending,
belief.

Two theologians for whom I have the utmost respect and admiration
in effect differ from each other here. George Caird once remarked to me:
"Probability has nothing to do with belief in the Christian faith." On the
other hand, Pannenberg observed in conversation: "This kind of remark
tends to divorce theology and faith from history and intellectual credibility.
This must not happen."[95] The complexity of the debate is reflected in the
controversial nature of the discussion about faith and history in theology and
in New Testament studies. Where there is a divorce or over-sharp dualism,
as in Martin Kähler or in Rudolf Bultmann, this is unacceptable. Many try
to achieve a more judicious balance, in which both sides make positive and
necessary points, and the debate advances. This still remains a live issue
among theologians today, with space for legitimate disagreement.

---

93. K. C. Flynn, "John Henry Newman, the Illative Sense, and the Threat of Scepticism"
(draft article online).

94. Wolterstorff, *John Locke*, 45–46.

95. Wolfhart Pannenberg, *Basic Questions in Theology* (London: SCM, 1970), 1.1–95.

PART II

FAITH

CHAPTER 4

Faith as Belief or Faith as Trust?

Belief and Trust in Biblical Languages and Thought

One momentous move in the history of Christian thought was the change from predominantly Greek terms to largely Latin ones in the Western church. On the subject of faith this had radical consequences. In Greek both the noun *pistis* and the verb *pisteuō* could denote either "belief" and "believing" (including "believing that or believing in") or "trust or trusting in." However, in Latin a choice had to be made between the noun *fides* ("faith") and the verb *credo* ("I believe"). The linguistic transfer caused a sharp difference between trust and belief. Many non-Latin languages retain the Greek merger: for example, the German *der Glaube* ("faith") is integrally related to *Glauben* ("to believe"). But in French "faith" (*la foi*) differs sharply from "believe" (*croire*). Thus Latin, French, and English force a choice that is not usually relevant in Greek and German.

The Hebrew terms predate the Greek, and they mostly but not always merge trust and belief. The broad use of *'mn* can generate *'ĕmûnâ* ("fidelity, faith, security"), *ne'ĕmān* ("faithful"), *'āmēn* ("faithful, true, so be it"), *'ōmen* ("fidelity, truth"), and *'ēmûn* ("faithful, fidelity"). The notion of trust is implicit in many of these terms, but Hebrew also uses *bāṭaḥ* ("to trust, confide in"; with other grammatical forms: "to feel secure, make secure, inspire confidence") and *beṭaḥ* ("confidence, safety, security"). For example, "trust in the LORD with all your heart, and do not rely on your own insight" (Prov. 3:5 NRSV) has Hebrew *bĕṭaḥ 'el-yhwh bĕkol-libbekā* ("not in your heart"). On the other hand, "if you do not stand firm in faith, you shall not stand"

(Isa. 7:9 NRSV) reflects Hebrew *'im lō' ta'ĕmînû*.[1] Brown, Driver and Briggs render the verb "trust or believe," almost at random, together with "believe in, be faithful, be confirmed, and stand firm."

Still more decisive comments of interpretation, however, come from Otto Michel and R. W. L. Moberly. The ancient Hebrews and many or most Greeks would have made little sense of the question of whether faith means trust or belief. In the oldest secular Greek the passive of *pisteuō* or *pistoō* may mean either "to be faithful" (or "to be bound") or "to be trusting or trustworthy" (Homer, *Odyssey* 21.217-18; *Iliad* 2.124; Hesiod, *Works* 372; and later in Sophocles, *Oedipus Rex* 625; Aeschylus, *Agamemnon* 651; and Xenophon, *Memorabilia* 4.4). In the Old Testament, as noted, *'mn* in many of its forms means "to be faithful" and can be applied to Moses (Num. 12:7), servants (1 Sam. 22:14), witnesses (Isa. 8:2), messengers (Prov. 25:13), and prophets (1 Sam. 3:20).[2] It also applies to the faithfulness or dependability of God (1 Kings 8:26; 1 Chron. 17:23-25). In such contexts it is often connected with believing God's promises as trustworthy or sure.

The root *bāṭaḥ* ("to trust") soon became assimilated to the meaning of *'mn* (Exod. 4:1-9, 27-31), and as Michel continues, it becomes a paradigm of belief and trust in response to Isaiah's call for trust when Ahaz and Hezekiah face the threat from Assyria. Isaiah declares: "if you do not stand firm in faith, you shall not stand" (Isa. 7:9 NRSV). Then Genesis 15:6 (Abraham "believed the LORD; and the LORD reckoned it to him as righteousness"; NRSV) is taken up and quoted in Romans 4:3, 9, 22-23 and Galatians 3:6. Moberly makes precisely the same point, adding Romans 1:17 and Hebrews 10:38.[3] Isaiah continues in 28:16: "Thus says the LORD God, See, I am laying in Zion a foundation stone, a tested stone, a precious cornerstone, a sure foundation: 'One who trusts will not panic'" (NRSV). The prophet himself, says Michel, is "an example of believing trust."[4] Faith and faithfulness also "stand here close together in the Heb[rew] term *'ĕmûnâ*."[5]

1. F. Brown, S. R. Driver, and C. A. Briggs, *Hebrew and English Lexicon of the Old Testament* (Lafayette: Associated Publishers, 1980), 52-54.

2. Otto Michel, "Faith," in *New International Dictionary of New Testament Theology*, ed. Colin Brown (Exeter: Paternoster, 1975), 1.595.

3. R. W. L. Moberly, "'ĕmûn," in *New International Dictionary of Old Testament Theology and Exegesis*, ed. Willem A. VanGemeren (Carlisle: Paternoster, 1996), 1.427-33 at 428.

4. Michel, "Faith," 596.

5. Ibid., 597.

The ground or, to use Alvin Plantinga's term, "warrant" for faith and believing is the covenant and the promises of God. The covenant serves precisely to offer security in our relation with God. Walther Eichrodt declares: "The fear of arbitrariness and caprice in the Godhead is excluded. With this God men know *exactly where they stand: an atmosphere of trust and security* is created, in which they find both the strength for a willing surrender to the will of God, and joyful courage to grapple with the problems of life."[6] On this basis "the covenant meal on the mount of God described in Exod. 24:9–11 lends further weight to such considerations."[7]

Similarly Moberly points out that both *'ĕmûnâ* ("reliable, faithful") and *bṭḥ* and *mibṭāḥ* ("trust") have *šeqer* ("falsehood, deception") as their semantic opposite. The passage in Psalm 115:9, "trust in the Lord" (NRSV), finds its ground in God as the rock (Isa. 26:3–4) and in the faithful God of promise.[8] The striking feature of promise is that the God of Israel is willing to bind himself, to restrict his freedom of choice, to be faithful to his promises. Both God's promise and God's commandment are trustworthy (Ps. 119:66).

In the New Testament even "believing that" followed by a preposition is not far removed from "trust in" and "believing in." For example, in Romans 10:9 Paul asserts: "'The word is near you, on your lips and in your hearts' . . . because if you confess with your lips that Jesus is Lord and believe in your heart that God raised him from the dead, you will be saved" (NRSV). Michel observes: "For Paul *pistis* is indissolubly bound with proclamation. Early Christian missionary preaching brought faith into sharp focus."[9] Galatians 2:16 offers a near parallel with "believe in": "We have come to believe in Christ" (NRSV). Here "believe in" and "trust in" have a close relationship to "believe in your heart that . . ." (Rom. 10:8–10). Similarly "since we believe that Jesus died and rose once again" is closely related to God's promise of resurrection in Christ (1 Thess. 4:14 NRSV).

In the same way, "I believe in" (Greek *pisteuō eis*) occurs not only in Galatians 2:16 ("we have come to believe in Christ") but also in John 1:12 ("to all who received him, who believed in his name"; NRSV) and John 3:18

---

6. Walther Eichrodt, *Theology of the Old Testament* (London: SCM, 1961), 1.38 (emphasis original).

7. Ibid., 1.43.

8. Moberly, "*'ĕmûn*," 431.

9. Michel, "Faith," 599.

("believed in the name of the only Son of God"; NRSV). Hebrews 6:1 per-
haps refers to an early Christian catechism: "Faith in [NRSV: toward] God"
(Greek *pisteōs epi theon*). Gerhard Barth argues that "faith" readily has the
meaning "trust" even when a variety of prepositions is used. Thus "have faith
in God" (Mark 11:22) is rendered by a simple objective genitive (*echete pistin
theou*). Hebrews 6:1 has *epi theon*; 1 Thessalonians 1:8 has *pros ton theon*; and
in 1 Peter 1:21 "you have come to trust in God" (NRSV) translates *pistous eis
theon*. Thus the Greek prepositions *eis*, *pros*, and *epi* with the simple objective
genitive may all have the force of "trust in."[10]

Gerhard Barth also asserts the general principle of my argument: "One
cannot proceed on the assumption of a uniform concept of faith standing at
the beginning of New Testament development, one that was then developed
in various ways." Nevertheless, he continues, in the New Testament the most
"central and comprehensive" designation is "an indissoluble relationship to
Jesus as the crucified and exalted Lord of the Church."[11] In this sense, as
Rudolf Bultmann also notes, what faith is finds its definition in to whom it is
related. This is why belief that, for example, God raised Jesus from the dead
is integrally related to believing in Jesus Christ, or trusting in him.

Faith or belief (*pistis*) certainly becomes a moment-by-moment stance
of trust in the Fourth Gospel. This becomes especially clear in Bultmann's
exposition of the vine and the branches (John 15:1-8).[12] He asserts that
"abiding" here is not "a limited, demonstrable, achievement," but a dynamic,
onward-moving, abiding, where "enough is never enough.... God ... con-
tinually demands something new from him [the believer].... Belonging to
him [Jesus] is itself the basis that creates movement.... Faith is that uncon-
ditional decision to base oneself on the act of God ... persistence in the life
of faith ... a *continued being ... from* [God]."[13]

If the New Testament blends belief and trust so evidently, what gave
rise to the widespread contrast between "trust/faith in" and "belief that"?
The answer is partly philosophical, where belief is often "belief that" fol-

10. Gerhard Barth, "*Pistis, Pisteuō*," in *Exegetical Dictionary of the New Testament*, ed.
Hoost Balz and Gerhard Schneider (Grand Rapids: Eerdmans, 1982-83), 3.91-98 at 93.
11. Ibid., 3.93.
12. Rudolf Bultmann, *The Gospel of John: A Commentary* (Oxford: Blackwell, 1971),
529-39.
13. Ibid., 533-35.

lowed by a proposition not a person. But in the New Testament the stance or disposition of belief or trust is also often based on acceptance and appropriation of a proposition (often biblical or credal) as the basis or warrant. The primary cause, however, is the point that I made at the beginning of this chapter. While the Greek (*pistis, pisteuō*) allows for an easy merger of the two concepts, Latin readily distinguished between faith (*fides*) and belief or believing (*credo*). Tertullian, Ambrose, and especially Augustine, like other Latin Fathers, wrote in Latin. Hence Kierkegaard placed the full weight of blame of this difference and confusion on Augustine. Furthermore, belief or faith in Christ himself involves a proposition about who Christ is, as Graham Stanton points out.[14]

Faith, Trust, Reason, and Fideism in Postbiblical Thought

Kierkegaard holds a mixed view of Augustine's theology and his influence in the history of Christian thought. On the one hand, he admires Augustine's emphasis on divine grace and human obedience, although he also firmly rejects Augustine's formulation. On the other hand, he writes in his *Journals*: "Augustine has done incalculable harm. The whole of Christian doctrine through the centuries really rests on him—and he has confused the concept of faith. . . . [He has made it] a concept which belongs to the sphere of the intellect. . . . From the Christian point of view faith belongs to the existential: God did not appear in the character of a professor, who has some doctrines which must first be believed, and then understood."[15]

Kierkegaard argues that Augustine had too readily drawn on the Platonic-Aristotelian concept of faith. He calls into question the whole rationalist understanding of faith from the early Christian apologists, through Clement of Alexandria, perhaps Origen, and Aquinas, to Descartes, Locke, and Hegel. Kierkegaard writes that even to talk *about* God in the third person brings its dangers. He comments: "They are busy about getting a truer and truer conception of God, but seem to forget the very first step, that one

14. Graham N. Stanton, *Jesus of Nazareth in New Testament Preaching*, Society for New Testament Studies Monograph 27 (Cambridge: Cambridge University Press, 1974).
15. Søren Kierkegaard, *The Last Years: Journals, 1853–55* (London: Collins, 1965), 99.

should fear God."[16] As Bultmann later observed, God addresses us; we do not speculate about him. In his well-known book *Attack upon "Christendom" 1854–1855*, Kierkegaard argues that Christendom has sided with the talkers and theorists: "Christianity . . . is repugnant to the natural man, is an offence to him. . . . He must revolt . . . by the help of a knavish trick, calling Christianity what is the exact opposite of Christianity, and then thanking God . . . for the great and inestimable privilege of being a Christian."[17]

In the same book Kierkegaard uses satire and irony to undermine the notion that faith is "the faith" of Danish state religion. He observes: "Christianity has been *abolished* by *expansion*, by those millions of name-Christians, the number of which is surely meant to conceal the fact that there is not one Christian. . . . This shoal of name-Christians, a Christian state, a Christian world, [are] notions shrewdly calculated to make God so confused in his head . . . that He cannot discover that He has been hoaxed, that there is not one single Christian."[18] His target is "Christian orthodoxy." As long as fees are paid for a Christian burial, he argues, "We are all Christians."[19] Faith has become evaporated into formal assent to "the faith." Protestantism, he says, especially in Denmark, has become "jovial mediocrity. . . . How could it occur to anyone that . . . Jesus Christ talks about the cross and agony and suffering, crucifying the flesh."[20] Christian education, he adds, is merely "learning a few things," not speaking of God in terms distinctive to New Testament Christianity.[21]

In more positive terms, Kierkegaard regards genuine faith as inviting us to tremble, because "God . . . is . . . so infinitely exalted," and we are "nothing in comparison with Him."[22] The difference between God and the world is such that a true Christian can be "hated by men because he is determined to be a Christian."[23] For faith must be lived out. In *The Point of View for My*

16. Søren Kierkegaard, *Concluding Unscientific Postscript* (Princeton: Princeton University Press, 1941), 484.

17. Søren Kierkegaard, *Attack upon "Christendom" 1854–1855* (London: Oxford University Press, 1946), 150.

18. Ibid., 127.

19. Ibid., 107.

20. Ibid., 34.

21. Ibid., 223.

22. Ibid., 255.

23. Ibid., 263.

Work as an Author, Kierkegaard writes: "The whole of my work as an author is related to . . . the problem of 'becoming a Christian,' with . . . polemic against the monstrous illusion we call Christendom."[24]

In Kierkegaard's view, faith is not just a "result," but a lived-out journey. He declares: "Truth becomes untruth in this or that person's mouth."[25] It would simply not be a confession of faith if a nontheist stated an orthodox christological formula or creed. His famous aphorism "truth is subjectivity" means that it involves personal, individual self-involvement and transformation as an "I."[26] In faith an individual "I" makes a firsthand decision and commitment for himself or herself. Abraham's faith in the face of the sacrifice of Isaac was a self-contradiction, not a rational instruction. Again Kierkegaard declares: "The most ruinous evasion of all is to be hidden in the crowd . . . in an attempt to get away from hearing God's voice as an individual."[27] Bultmann's later sermon "Adam, Where Art Thou?" makes precisely this point. The "how" of faith is "the passion of the infinite" in contrast to the objective nature of propositions or mere description.[28] Like Luther, he regards faith as "staking one's life, which one avoids doing if he [God] is a third person."[29]

Kierkegaard may certainly be regarded as a fideist. But fideism is a very broad term that covers a spectrum of meanings. At the weaker end of the spectrum it asserts the primacy of faith over reason. In this respect Blaise Pascal, Karl Barth, possibly Augustine, and even, according to some, Aquinas may loosely be regarded as fideists. But at the stronger end of the spectrum, it is suggested that Christian faith is *contrary* to reason, rather than simply *beyond* reason. In this respect Kierkegaard and possibly Tertullian are generally said to be fideist; while Aquinas was definitely not one.

Blaise Pascal (1623–62) had already established his reputation as a scientist and mathematician when he underwent a direct and personal experience of Christ in 1654. It is noteworthy that he never questioned the validity of reason for his scientific endeavors, and specifically urged that reason was *not*

24. Søren Kierkegaard, *The Point of View for My Work as an Author* (Oxford: Oxford University Press, 1939; repr. New York: Harper, 1962), 5–6.

25. Kierkegaard, *Concluding Unscientific Postscript*, 181.

26. Ibid., 169.

27. Søren Kierkegaard, *Purity of Heart Is to Will One Thing* (London: Fontana, 1961), 163.

28. Kierkegaard, *Concluding Unscientific Postscript*, 181.

29. Søren Kierkegaard, *The Last Years: Journals, 1853–55* (London: Collins, 1965), 533.

contrary to Christian faith or religion. Indeed reason could be used against what he called "careless skepticism." Some call him a fideist primarily because in his *Pensées* (1670) he referred to "reasons of the heart." Thus for many the application of the term to Pascal remains questionable.

The application of the term "fideism" to Tertullian (ca. 160–225) is less controversial. He converted from paganism to Christianity in middle life and subsequently produced many treatises in Latin, of which over thirty survive. One of his most memorable sayings was "what has Jerusalem to do with Athens?" comparing biblical revelation with Greek philosophy.[30] In this same chapter he calls Greek philosophy "the doctrines of men and demons," which the Lord called "foolishness" (1 Cor. 3:18–19), citing Heraclitus, Zeno, Aristotle, and others. He asks: "What concord is there between the Academy and the Church?" Murphy, Mezei, and Oakes contrast Tertullian's view that faith conflicts with philosophy with that of his contemporary, Clement of Alexandria (ca. 150–ca. 215). Clement insisted on their positive compatibility.[31] On the other hand, Tertullian drew on Stoic philosophy for his view of the soul. In this treatise he claims biblical warrant for his view and rejects Plato's account.[32]

In modern times a broad understanding of fideism is often applied to the "dialectical theology" of the 1920s. These thinkers included Karl Barth, Friedrich Gogarten, E. Thurneysen, Emil Brunner, and at the time Rudolf Bultmann. Reason, they believed, would not allow direct assertions about the transcendent God, but there was still room, they argued, for a dialectical "yes" and "no" of assertions. Barth's second edition of his commentary on Romans (1922) owed much to Kierkegaard's influence. God was both hidden and revealed. Although he rejected "natural theology" less emphatically, Brunner allowed for what he called "eristics," which he defined as "the intellectual discussion of the Christian faith in the light of [approaches] which are opposed to the Christian message."[33] Brunner used "eristics" in contrast to the broader term "apologetics," in spite of overlaps of the two terms.

Karl Barth (1886–1968) reacted strongly against the quasi-intellectual

---

30. Tertullian, *Prescriptions against Heretics* 7 (*ANF* 3.246).

31. Francesca A. Murphy, Balázs M. Mezei, and Kenneth Oakes, *Illuminating Faith* (London/New York: Bloomsbury, 2015), 9–10.

32. Tertullian, *On the Soul* (*ANF* 3.181–235).

33. Emil Brunner, *The Christian Doctrine of God* (London: Lutterworth, 1949), 98.

approach of classical liberalism, such as that of Harnack and Jülicher. He expounded, instead, "The Strange New World of the Bible," with "not right human thoughts about God, but right divine thoughts about persons."[34] God is other than humankind. A key to the *Church Dogmatics* (1932–67) was his reading of Anselm, and the interpretation was published as *Anselm: Fides Quaerens Intellectum* (1930).[35] Barth regarded the word of God as coming to us as address, act, and gift, not as a body of propositions open to value-neutral enquiry. In his second German volume on God, he declares: "God is known by God and by God alone."[36] God, he says, is ready to be known, but only when he chooses, and in God's way; knowledge of God depends on "his good pleasure."[37] Hence the problem of natural theology, or reason's access alone to God, is "grounded mischievously deep. "[38] Reason cannot climb up to God; God's grace descends from above in a contrary direction.

"Objectivity," Barth declares, comes not by the scientific method of the Enlightenment, but by revelation in accordance with the "object" of revelation. Religiosity and religious aspiration are no more capable than reason of reaching God through their "upward" motion; God's own word comes "from above." Indeed in 1934 in Rome, Barth expressed his disagreement with Brunner in his well-known book simply entitled *No*. Brunner had argued that without some common meeting point, such phenomena as repentance and the ordinance of marriage would lose their grounding. Barth replied that everything depended on the self-revelation of God. There is, for Barth, no "point of contact" (German *Anknüpfungspunkt*).[39] Following Anselm, he spoke of "faith seeking understanding." We cannot even argue on the basis of analogy. For God is revealed, Barth believed, not through an analogy of being (Latin *analogia entis*), but through an analogy of faith (*analogia fidei*).

Today the most direct representatives of Barth's theology are probably Eberhard Jüngel (born 1934); two very sympathetic expositors in Britain: Thomas F. Torrance (1913–2007) and John Webster (born 1955); and George

34. Karl Barth, *The Word of God and the Word of Man* (London: Hodder & Stoughton, 1928), 43.

35. Karl Barth, *Church Dogmatics* (Grand Rapids: Eerdmans/Edinburgh: T&T Clark, 1936–75).

36. Ibid., 3.179.

37. Ibid., 3.63, 74.

38. Ibid., 3.135.

39. Ibid., 1.273.

Hunsinger of Princeton.[40] Fideism, however, remains an elastic term, and we should be cautious about its application to given thinkers, without very careful qualification.

Faith and Reason in Biblical and Patristic Writers

Those thinkers who believe in the compatibility of faith and reason cover perhaps an even greater spectrum of views. Augustine and Aquinas regarded them as compatible, but had reservations about the capacity of human reason without faith to find God. Wolfhart Pannenberg strongly advocates the use of reason and rational argument in theology, not least to defend its credibility in the university and public arena. Alvin Plantinga and Nicholas Wolterstorff also regard the compatibility of reason and faith as vital, but within the definitions and beliefs of Reformed epistemology. Most Catholic theologians reflect the tradition of Aquinas, but modern research suggests different nuances of interpretation. If we go back to John Locke, he saw reason as our guide in all things, yet was clearly a man of faith.

First, we may return to biblical evidence on this subject, especially to Paul. It is a popular misconception that Paul underrated human reason. Admittedly, completely on its own, human reason could indeed diverge from "the wisdom of God" and constitute "foolishness" (1 Cor. 3:18; cf. 1:18, 20, 23). Reason is also narrower than wisdom in the Old Testament and Pauline tradition, where wisdom includes the corporate and cumulative wisdom of the generations. But in Romans 12:2 he urges transformation "by the renewing of your minds, so that you may discern what is the will of God" (NRSV). Ephesians 4:23 repeats this: "Be renewed in the spirit of your minds" (NRSV; Greek *ananeousthai tō pneumati tou voos*), where Danker renders *nous* as "an attitude of mind."[41] In 1 Corinthians 14:14-15 Paul wishes the mind to be intelligently engaged and not unfruitful. In Romans 1:28 the minds of sinful

---

40. John Webster (ed.), *The Cambridge Companion to Karl Barth* (Cambridge: Cambridge University Press, 2000). Cf. Thomas Torrance, *Theological Science* (London: Oxford University Press, 1969) and numerous other works; Eberhard Jüngel, *God as the Mystery of the World* (Edinburgh: T&T Clark, 1983); George Hunsinger, *How to Read Karl Barth* (Oxford: Oxford University Press, 1991) and *Disruptive Grace* (Grand Rapids: Eerdmans, 2004).

41. BDAG 680.

pagans have been darkened. In Romans 14:5 a Christian must be convinced in his own mind. Most of all, in Galatians 3:1, Paul beseeches the Galatians not to be "foolish," by failing to use their minds to see the implication of their experience of the Spirit: "Are you so foolish? Having started with the Spirit, are you now ending with the flesh? Did you experience so much for nothing?" (3:3–4 NRSV).

Robert Jewett, Gunther Bornkamm, and especially Stanley K. Stowers demonstrate beyond doubt the value that Paul places on the mind.[42] Bornkamm points out that "mind" also takes up and includes the intellectual dimension of the Old Testament term "heart."[43] He continues: "Paul speaks of reason . . . in order to convict the hearer of his guilt before God. . . . The mind manifests to man his separation from God."[44] He adds: "Paul allots to reason and to the rationality of men an exceedingly important role for the self-understanding of the Christian and for all areas of his life." He also anticipates Pannenberg in declaring: "The style of the Pauline sermon is just *not* that of revelation-speech [e.g., 'Thus says the Lord . . .'] but of the diatribe, . . . a manner of speaking which regards the hearer as a partner in dialogue. . . . The message is to be *understood*."[45] The theme of reason, he says, has an important role in Paul's ethical directives. Ethical directives were long familiar to rational critics of paganism.

Robert Jewett is no less emphatic. He first traces early modern research, and later modern work, from Bultmann to Stacey. He then stresses the polemic context of 1–2 Thessalonians (1 Thess. 5:12, 14; 2 Thess. 3:15). It may be, Jewett suggests, that the "pneumatic enthusiasts . . . were sometimes 'out of their minds' in various sorts of ecstatic experiences."[46] This was certainly the case, he argues, in Galatians, where the converts had been "bewitched" (Gal. 3:1). Paul calls them to use their minds. In addition to his "Paul on the Use and Abuse of Reason," Stowers also gives many examples of Paul's use of the diatribe form, especially in Romans (2:1–16, 17–29; 3:1–8, 9–20, 27–31; 4:1–12;

---

42. Stanley K. Stowers, "Paul on the Use and Abuse of Reason," in *Greeks, Romans, Christians*, ed. D. L. Balch et al. (Minneapolis: Fortress, 1990), 253–86.

43. Gunther Bornkamm, "Faith and Reason in Paul," in Bornkamm's *Early Christian Experience* (London: SCM, 1969), 29–46 at 32.

44. Ibid., 35.

45. Ibid., 36, 38.

46. Robert Jewett, *Paul's Anthropological Terms* (Leiden: Brill, 1971), 369.

5:12–21; 6:1–14, 15–23; 9:30–10:4) and elsewhere.[47] This, again, favors Paul's use of argument, rather than declarative revelation-speech. Jewett endorses this in his commentary on Romans.[48]

After the close of the New Testament era, the next clear examples of the compatibility of faith and reason were the early Christian apologists. Aristides and Quadratus (early second century) addressed Hadrian or more probably Antoninus Pius. The most well known, however, was Justin Martyr (ca. 100–ca. 165), who wrote two "apologies" or defenses of the faith. Both use rational argument. In the *First Apology* (ca. 155) he argues that some people unjustly accused Christians of atheism; this accusation was unjust, since Christians offer hymns of thanksgiving to God, pray for their enemies, and reject idolatry.[49] In his *Second Apology* (ca. 161) he replies to more unjust accusation against Christians, pointing out that even Socrates had been unjustly accused.[50] In his *Dialogue with Trypho* he offers a sustained comparison by rational argument between Christianity and Judaism.

Justin's pupil Tatian argued for a righteous life and obedience to wisdom.[51] Athenagoras of Athens addressed his *Embassy on Behalf of Christians* to the Emperor Marcus Aurelius and his son Commodus. He argued first that God created all things and holds them together by his Spirit.[52] (Spirit would have been a familiar term to Marcus Aurelius.) Then he proceeds to mount a series of arguments against unjust accusations against Christians.[53] Bishop Theophilus of Antioch argued for the rationality of the Christian view of creation, as against pagan myths of the Greco-Roman deities, and expounded the intelligibility and rationality of the Logos through God's Son, God's Wisdom, and God's Spirit.[54]

Clement of Alexandria (ca. 150–ca. 215) made use of pagan literature, including pagan philosophy, in his arguments in defense of the Christian

---

47. Stanley K. Stowers, *The Diatribe and Paul's Letter to the Romans*, Society of Biblical Literature Dissertation Series 57 (Chico: Scholars Press, 1981).

48. Robert Jewett, *Romans: A Commentary*, Hermeneia (Minneapolis: Fortress, 2007), esp. 25–27.

49. Justin, *First Apology* 1.3–8, 13 (*ANF* 1.166–67).

50. Justin, *Second Apology* 2.10 (*ANF* 1.193).

51. Tatian, *Against the Greeks* 16 (*ANF* 2.72).

52. Athenagoras, *Embassy on Behalf of Christians* 6 (*ANF* 2.132).

53. Ibid., 7–32 (*ANF* 2.132–48).

54. Theophilus, *Autolycus* 1.7 (*ANF* 2.91).

faith. At times he finds common cause with Homer and regards philosophy as the handmaid of theology, as "conducive to piety," and as "perfected in Christ."[55] He cites Solomon as directing us to wisdom: "Wisdom is the queen of philosophy, as philosophy is of preparatory culture."[56] It offers "previous training" to the Christian. It paves the way for divine virtue, provided that we draw only the best from Plato, Aristotle, and the Stoics.[57] Jesus said, "Seek and you shall find," which for Clement seemed to advocate open inquiry. He continues: "Truth is one," and there is a germ of truth in most philosophies.[58] Philosophers have gained some portion of the truth, for example, that God created the world, as Paul admits in Acts 17.[59] Plato was an imitator of Moses in framing laws.[60] Yet, for all that, knowledge of God can be obtained only through faith.[61] Augustine of Hippo (354–430) began in his earlier years after Christian conversion to speak of faith as instrumental to knowledge and understanding. This, some argue, applies to his *Confessions*, written in 397. But in later works, especially *The City of God* (413–26), he had "a new phase."[62] Murphy, Mezei, and Oakes call the first phase "instrumental faith," which leads to knowledge and understanding. It is underpinned by both authority and reason. Yet "Augustine never really sees faith as purely intellectual."[63] In the second phase faith becomes increasingly personal, when Augustine speaks of "the eyes of faith."[64] Faith becomes, in effect, contemplation. In Augustine, as in the New Testament, faith is never simply a human emotion.

Manicheans believed that faith was compatible with reason. But although in early years he came under the influence of the Manichees, Augustine gradually became disillusioned with their teaching. In his later opposition to Donatism (the doctrine of a "pure" church), Augustine allowed that faith could be fallible and make mistakes. Against the background of the Pelagian controversy he regarded faith emphatically as a gift of God. There

---

55. Clement of Alexandria, *Stromata* 1.4–5 (*ANF* 2.304–5).

56. Ibid., 1.5 (*ANF* 2.306).

57. Ibid., 1.7 (*ANF* 2.308).

58. Ibid., 1.13 (*ANF* 2.313).

59. Ibid., 1.19 (*ANF* 2.321).

60. Ibid., 1.25 (*ANF* 2.338).

61. Ibid., 2.2 (*ANF* 2.348).

62. Murphy, Mezei, and Oakes, *Illuminating Faith*, 10.

63. Ibid., 12.

64. Augustine, *The City of God* 14.9 (*NPNF¹* 2.269).

are at least three distinct contexts, therefore, in which Augustine developed his understanding of faith. Any totally systematic account is in danger of overlooking the complexity of his development in relation to these contexts. In his very early *Soliloquies* (386–87), for example, Augustine regards God as "the God of truth"; and he dialogues with others about reflection in the light of reason.[65] Yet he also speaks of faith as "rousing us to God": "It is by faith that we find you [God]."[66] In *The City of God* he asserts that the believer is justified by faith, in the sense of trusting and hoping in God.[67] In *On the Spirit and the Letter*, one of the Anti-Pelagian writings, Augustine writes: "The very will by which we believe is reckoned as a gift of God, because it arises out of the free will which we received at our creation."[68] Also in his work *On the Predestination of the Saints*, he writes: "Faith, then, as well in its beginning as in its completion, is God's gift."[69]

Hence, as in Scripture, faith has various meanings in the works of Augustine, or is polymorphous, depending on context. Augustine did not regard reason as self-sufficient, but he does regard it as a gift of God. Faith and reason are not incompatible. Reason may have a role in assisting belief in the testimony of prophets, apostles, and believers, yet "it is not sufficient for faith. . . . [Faith] is infused through a supernatural illumination, and is a gift of grace that sufficed for salvation."[70]

65. Augustine, *Soliloquies* 1.1 (*NPNF¹* 7.537).

66. Ibid., 1.3, 6 (*NPNF¹* 7.538–39).

67. Augustine, *The City of God* 10.25 (*NPNF¹* 2.195–96).

68. Augustine, *On the Spirit and the Letter* 60 (*NPNF¹* 5.110).

69. Augustine, *On the Predestination of the Saints* 16 (*NPNF¹* 5.506).

70. John R. T. Lamont, *Divine Faith* (Aldershot/Burlington: Ashgate, 2004), 51.

CHAPTER 5

Faith, Reason, and Argument in Biblical and Modern Thought

Faith, Reason, and Argument from Aquinas to Pannenberg

Thomas Aquinas (1225–74), strictly speaking, belongs to the medieval period, not to modern thought. However, one major difference from the earlier medieval period is the advent of the universities and the change from monastic and diocesan training to university institutions. Although he began his education as a Dominican monk, Aquinas was probably one of the first thinkers to reflect his university education. In Paris, Albert the Great introduced him to the works of Aristotle, whose writings had been newly translated from Arabic into Latin. The philosophers of Islam—Averroes, Al-Ghazali, and Avicenna—became familiar to him, as well as the Bible, Augustine, and Aristotle himself. In Paris, Aquinas wrote the whole *Summa Contra Gentiles* for missionaries among Muslims and then began his magisterial classic *Summa Theologiae*, which occupied him almost continuously until his death. This has become a classic textbook of systematic theology and remains a set text even today in the Roman Catholic Church.

Aquinas adopted an intellectualist approach to faith, although his respect for reason in no way undermined or excluded the need for revelation. Knowledge (Latin *scientia*) constituted more than mere opinion. It is self-evidently true and is also what can be demonstrated by inference. Faith, he believed, could not be demonstrated in the same way. Nevertheless he insisted on the rationality of faith; the Christian faith is compatible with rational enquiry and reflection.

Whereas Kierkegaard and Barth rejected the efficacy or relevance of the traditional arguments for the existence of God (at least as arguments), Aquinas formulated his "five ways." He writes: "There are five ways in which one can prove there is a God."[1] The first three of the five arguments amount to versions of the cosmological argument for the existence of God. The first concerns "change" (Latin *motum* and *moveat*) and actuality; the second relates to the nature of causation and "first cause" and the impossibility of an infinite chain of causes (*ad infinitum*); and the third way concerns contingency and necessity (*necessarium*).[2] The fourth way is the argument from degrees of being to the superlative; while the fifth way is the argument from design, or the teleological argument (in Aquinas's terms, the argument from "the guided-ness of nature" [*ex gubernatione rerum*]).[3]

Aquinas prefaces these arguments, however, with a proviso: "That God exists cannot . . . be made evident. For that God exists is an article of faith, and . . . faith is concerned with the unseen. . . . It is impossible to demonstrate that God exists."[4] Later in the *Summa* Aquinas moves on to discuss knowledge of God and declares: "It is impossible that any created mind should see the essence of God by his own natural powers."[5] On the contrary, he quotes 1 Corinthians 2:8, 10: "God has revealed to us through his Spirit . . . wisdom which none of this world rulers knew."[6]

Commenting on Aquinas's *Summa Contra Gentiles*, F. C. Copleston suggests: "One of Aquinas's aims was to show that the Christian faith rests on a rational foundation, and that the principles of philosophy do not necessarily lead to a view of the world which excludes Christianity."[7] In the *Summa Theologiae*, however, Aquinas complements this: "God [is] the guarantor of all truth. For the faith of which we are speaking does not assent to anything except insofar as it is revealed by God."[8] Aquinas distinguishes between *what*

1. Thomas Aquinas, *Summa Theologiae* (London: Eyre & Spottiswoode/New York: McGraw Hill, 1963), §2.13.1a Q2 art. 3.
2. Ibid., §2.12–15.1a Q2 art. 3.
3. Ibid., §2.14–17.1a Q2 art. 3.
4. Ibid., §2.8–9.1a Q2 art. 2.
5. Ibid., §2.8–9.1a Q12 art. 4 reply.
6. Ibid., §2.8–9.1a Q12 art. 13 and Q57 art. 5.
7. F. C. Copleston, *Aquinas: An Introduction to the Life and Work of the Great Mediaeval Thinker* (London: Penguin, 1955), 11–12.
8. Aquinas, *Summa Theologiae* §1.13–15.1a Q1 art. 3.

we believe, which is the domain of faith, and *by what means* we believe, which may involve intellect, inference, demonstration, and reason. Reason alone could never discover God as Trinity nor as the author of salvation, but it may assist us in arriving at belief in God as Creator.

Martin Luther (1483–1546) held, in general, a lower view of reason than Calvin. In fact in his voluminous writings it is easy to find some quotations that appear to disparage reason and others that praise its value. His view of reason is, in some respects, controversial. Brian Gerrish in his book *Grace and Reason* recognizes this, not least because both Luther's relation to nominalism and the exact nature of nominalism itself are far from clear.[9] Richard Dawkins, the popular atheistic scientist (or scientific journalist), relishes the well-known (or notorious) alleged quotation from Luther: "Reason is the greatest enemy that faith has; it never comes to the aid of the divine word, treating with contempt all that emanates from God."[10] But many, including Simon Sutherland, regard this quotation as problematic, suggesting that it probably comes from Luther's *Table Talk*, which was composed from memory by Luther's students, not by Luther himself.[11] On the other hand, as Pannenberg recalls, Luther would not call reason a monster, "the source of evil," or "the blind whore of the devil," except when it was used in very special contexts, such as his attack on the worst of medieval scholasticism.[12]

Other negative quotations are attributed to Luther. He is alleged to have called reason "Aristotle's evil brew." Nevertheless, on the other side, like Paul, he regarded reason as having a high value in reaching ethical decisions and an "indispensable guide to life and learning." His concern for the intellectual and theological education of priests is widely known. He regularly appealed to "arguments from reason and from Scripture."[13] When he studied the scripture, Luther "thinks . . . ponders . . . weighs it." Luther seems to be anticipating both the negative and positive aspects noted in Gunther Born-

---

9. Brian A. Gerrish, *Grace and Reason: A Study in the Theology of Martin Luther* (Oxford: Clarendon, 1962), 5.

10. Richard Dawkins, *The God Delusion* (Boston: Houghton Mifflin, 2006), 190.

11. Martin Luther, *Table Talks*, Luther's Works 54 (St. Louis: Concordia, 1967).

12. Wolfhart Pannenberg, *Basic Questions in Theology* (London: SCM, 1971), 2.48; and Martin Luther, *Luther's Works* (Philadelphia/St. Louis: Concord, 1955–), 40.175.

13. Theodore G. Tappert, *Luther: Letters of Spiritual Counsel*, Library of Christian Classics 18 (London: SCM, 1965), 149.

kamm's essay "Faith and Reason in Paul."[14] Among Luther's disciples and friends, Melanchthon is widely understood as concerned with systematic and coherent argument in his *Loci Communes* of 1521. Yet at the same time Melanchthon regarded faith as trust in the promises and mercy of God. Reason has an even higher role among Lutheran scholastics, for example, in Johannes Andreas Quenstadt (1617–88).

John Calvin (1509–64) certainly agreed that humans distinguish between good and evil by reason, even if human sin partly (but not wholly) has corrupted and distorted reason. Calvin writes: "To charge the intellect with perpetual blindness. . . . It is repugnant . . . to the Word of God. . . . We have one kind of intelligence of earthly things, another of heavenly things."[15] The latter relates to God and his kingdom; the former to righteousness and "some principle of civil order."[16] Reason distinguishes humans from brute beasts.[17] Admittedly he also quotes: "No man can say that Jesus is Lord, but by the Holy Ghost" (1 Cor. 12:3).[18] But reason is useful in "regulating conduct."[19] Moreover the apostle Paul prays for the renewal of the mind, and mind or reason is a part of the human heart, which Calvin especially emphasized as central.

Apart from such comments, however, Calvin's appreciation of reason can be seen in broader approach in the *Institutes* and in his careful historical and linguistic exegesis in his many commentaries. In his work on Calvin's commentaries, Joseph Harmoutunian includes a section on faith and reason and Calvin. On one side, he writes: "Faith, which is the proper work of the Spirit, must rely upon, and draw its strength from, the promise of God in Christ and Scripture."[20] On the other side: "Faith did not solve the problem raised by reason to reason's satisfaction. . . . Faith is the knowledge of God's goodness toward his suffering people."[21] In Calvin's comments on Titus 1:1:

14. Gunther Bornkamm, "Faith and Reason in Paul," in Bornkamm's *Early Christian Experience* (London: SCM, 1969), 29–46 at 32.

15. John Calvin, *Institutes of the Christian Religion*, ed. H. Beveridge (London: James Clarke, 1957), 1.234 §2.2.12–13.

16. Ibid., 2.235 §2.2.13.

17. Ibid., 2.237 §2.2.17.

18. Ibid., 2.239 §2.2.20.

19. Ibid., 2.241 §2.2.22.

20. Joseph Harmoutunian (ed.), *Calvin's Commentaries*, Library of Christian Classics 23 (London: SCM, 1958), 43.

21. Ibid., 44.

Paul "calls faith knowledge ... by saying that it is of the essence of faith to know the truth, he plainly shows that there is certainly no faith without knowledge."[22]

John Locke (1632–1704) needs no extended discussion here since I already considered his views on belief in some detail. In 1695 he published *The Reasonableness of Christianity*, in which reasonableness is not equated with rationality. Later he claimed that a reasonable belief is one that the believer is entitled to believe. In his *Essay concerning Human Understanding* (1690), his aim was to enquire into the origins of certainty, "the grounds and degrees of belief, opinion, and assent," and to provide "a cure for scepticism."[23] He recognized that the human mind shaped what he called "secondary" qualities, such as color, but not the world of empirical realities such as solidity and extension.[24] Locke also discussed human identity in his famous parable of the soul of the prince who entered the body of the cobbler.[25] He also attacked purely psychological certainty as "enthusiasm" in book 4.19.

Although ideas come especially through the five senses, as the major empiricists agreed, reflection transforms simple ideas into complex ones, not least through inference and by evaluating probabilities. One of the longest chapters in Locke's book 4 is chapter 18, entitled "Of Reason." He first discusses the various meanings of reason, allowing that "men can reason well, who cannot make a syllogism."[26] He adds: "Our reason often fails us."[27] Indeed he concludes: "*Reason and faith are not opposite, for faith must be regulated by reason.* There is another use of the word *reason* wherein it is opposed to faith—(but this is) a very improper way of speaking."[28]

The Enlightenment is difficult to date precisely, not least because the dating may be viewed differently in England, France, and Germany. Immanuel Kant in Germany defined the Enlightenment (German *Aufklärung*) as "man's exodus from his [man's] self-incurred tutelage," that is, to use one's own un-

---

22. Calvin, *Calvin's Commentaries: The Second Epistle of Paul to the Corinthians and the Epistles of Paul to Timothy, Titus, and Philemon* (Edinburgh: Oliver & Boyd/St. Andrew Press, 1964), 352.

23. Locke, *Essay*, 1.1.1 (and 1.1.3, 6).

24. Ibid., 2.8.9.

25. Ibid., 2.27.

26. Ibid., 4.18.4.

27. Ibid., 4.18.9.

28. Ibid., 4.18.24 (emphasis added).

derstanding. According to Enlightenment thought, one must throw off any dependence upon authorities and traditions in order to think for oneself. But the Enlightenment began much earlier than Kant. Many writers today associate the Enlightenment especially with the English Deists and the French Encyclopedists. Although several theorists claim to have been inspired by Locke, a number of Enlightenment thinkers did not share his Christian faith. Indeed Reventlow attributes most non-Christian ideas in radical biblical criticism to the influence of the Deists in the broadly secular Enlightenment.[29] In France the Encyclopedists included Denis Diderot (1713–84) and Voltaire (1694–1778). Diderot specifically adopted an anti-Christian position. La Mettrie's book *Man the Machine* (1747) sums up their atheistic philosophy. In Germany Samuel Reimarus (1694–1768) rejected every concept of the supernatural. English Deists included John Toland (1670–1722), Matthew Tindal (1655–1733), and Anthony Collins (1676–1729). Collins argued that freethinking must be independent of any authority and tradition.

Enlightenment thought dominated the sciences and much of theology until at least the early part of the twentieth century, or perhaps longer. From 1960 onward, however, such philosophers as Hans-Georg Gadamer (1900–2002) raised fundamental questions about the status and presuppositions of the Enlightenment, including its obsession with human reason. This occurred not only in the natural sciences, but also especially in hermeneutics, philosophy, and the social sciences. Gadamer argues: "The focus of objectivity [of the human mind or consciousness] is a distorting mirror. The self-awareness of the individual is only a flickering in the closed circuits of historical life."[30] Karl-Otto Apel, Jürgen Habermas, and others express reservations about Enlightenment rationalism.

Georg W. F. Hegel (1770–1831) anticipated Gadamer in his emphasis on historical understanding and historical reason, but differed from him in also giving great importance to the rational as such. He opposed subjectivism in Schelling and instrumentalism in Kant, but stressed instead Absolute Mind or Absolute Spirit (German *Geist*) and the universal principle of reason. Hegel claimed that reason is reality, and reality is reason: "In thinking I

29. Henning Graf Reventlow, *The Authority of the Bible and the Rise of the Modern World* (London: SCM, 1984), 383 and passim.

30. Hans-Georg Gadamer, *Truth and Method*, 2nd ed. (London: Sheed & Ward, 1989), 276.

lift myself up into the Absolute."[31] Along these lines, Hegel believed that the Christian doctrine of the Trinity arose from the historical unfolding of God, or the Absolute, in history, logic, and reason, to become (in finite thought) God the Father, God the Son, and God the Holy Spirit. Faith and reason, he concluded, are entirely compatible. Whether his doctrine of the Holy Trinity emerged as an inference of his logic or as an inference from theology is often debated.

In more recent thought Carl Michalson applies Hegel's historical reason to faith in his book *The Rationality of Faith*.[32] Much of his book concerns "the historical form of faith" and "the rationality of historicity." He believes that Christian theology should be open to philosophy, reason, and history, but perhaps tends to obscure what many call the supernatural. He advocates the importance of rationality within the bounds of history.

Gerhard Ebeling (1912–2001) is among those who stress that faith both entails commitment and must have intellectual foundations. Questions about faith can make sense only if we include commitment as part of the questions, and yet "there can be no faith without understanding. . . . To understand . . . certain knowledge is essential."[33] We must not, he says, let faith be dissolved "in mood and feeling."[34]

Wolfhart Pannenberg (1928–2014) is our last and perhaps clearest example of a thinker who argues for the importance of reason for Christian faith. He virtually single-handedly moved theology away from the dominance of existentialism and subjectivism of Martin Heidegger and Rudolf Bultmann. He also shows affinity with many of Hegel's ideas, although with careful moderation, sobriety, and distinct modifications. Pannenberg has a high regard for both history and rationality. But he also sees that many "historical-critical procedures" in biblical studies, for example, were "guilty of anthropocentricity."[35] He regards history as "the most comprehensive horizon of Christian theology."[36]

---

31. Georg W. F. Hegel, *Lectures in the Philosophy of Religion* (London: Kegan Paul, 1895), 1.63.

32. Carl Michalson, *The Rationality of Faith* (London: SCM, 1964).

33. Gerhard Ebeling, *The Nature of Faith* (London: Collins, 1961), 10, 12, 14.

34. Ibid., 20.

35. Wolfhart Pannenberg, *Basic Questions in Theology* (London: SCM, 1970), 1.39.

36. Ibid., 1.25.

Pannenberg's classic essay, "Faith and Reason," comes in volume 2 of *Basic Questions in Theology*. He recognizes that "a rational account of the truth of faith has acquired an ever more acute urgency in the modern period."[37] Like Locke, he recognizes that reason is not a uniformly determined entity. Luther, for example, spoke often of the Aristotelian concept of reason. We should take account of this in evaluating Aquinas, Luther, and Kant. Pannenberg continues: "Faith, on the other hand, is directed towards something future, or toward him who promises and guarantees something *future*" (Heb. 11:1).[38] He adds that historical reason is by no means merely a theoretical concept, and he refers approvingly to Hegel and Dilthey in this respect. Only from the point of view of the end of history can reality fully make sense.[39]

In his essay "Insight and Faith," Pannenberg argues that Paul grounds faith in knowledge (Rom. 6:8–9; 2 Cor. 4:13). We cannot escape the role of reason, he declares, by appealing to the Holy Spirit: "*An otherwise unconvincing message cannot attain the power to convince simply by appealing to the Holy Spirit.*"[40] It is rather, he declares, that speaking in the Spirit has credibility by its testimony to Christ (1 Cor. 12:3). He continues: "The Holy Spirit becomes effective *through his [the preacher's] words and arguments. Argument and the operation of the Spirit are not in competition with each other.*"[41] In his later book *Theology and the Philosophy of Science*, Pannenberg speaks of the importance of the public credibility of theology and the "truth of Christianity by generally accepted criteria."[42] This emerged especially in the thirteenth century with the rise of the earliest universities and a "shared concept of truth."

The importance of such rationality, however, does not suggest that truth about God can be anything other than contingent. Pannenberg rejects the notion that the truth of God is "exalted above all time" or timeless.[43] "In a contingent manner," he says, "does not mean absolutely 'irrational,' but rather

37. Ibid., 2.53.
38. Ibid., 2.58 (emphasis added).
39. Ibid., 2.61–64.
40. Ibid., 2.34 (emphasis added).
41. Ibid., 2.35 (emphasis added).
42. Wolfhart Pannenberg, *Theology and the Philosophy of Science* (Philadelphia: Westminster, 1976), 13.
43. Pannenberg, *Basic Questions*, 2.5.

that *contingent* events are the basis of a *historical* experience."[44] Hence he also remains respectful of hermeneutics and of Hegel. Indeed his most serious difference from Hegel was that "the proleptic character of the destiny of Jesus is the basis for the openness to the future for us, despite the fact that Jesus is the ultimate revelation of the God of Israel as the God of all men."[45] Thus in the context of history and of apocalyptic, he stresses the importance of argumentation. Paul, he pointed out, could have spared himself the trouble of much argumentation, if he had been willing simply to write, "Thus says the Lord," as the introduction to each epistle. This would have been a revelation speech, not a careful argument of persuasive discourse.

T. F. Torrance makes a similar point. Faith is fully rational, but also embraces the Holy Spirit: "Knowledge of God takes place not only within the rational structures, but also within the personal and social structures of human life, where the Spirit is at work *as personalizing* Spirit."[46]

From these many examples we may conclude that reason retains a complex relation to faith, depending on the character of each. Not only do doubt, faith, and certainty vary in meaning depending on their context, but the same can also be said of reason. As Locke argued, reasonableness is not rationalism. But in many circumstances and for many purposes we may conclude that authentic Christian faith is not antirational and that reason may play definite, though limited, roles in its grounding. We must resist the postmodern fashion of relying only on narrative and testimony, as if reason had no place for faith in arriving at truth.

Vatican II and Pope John Paul II

We may first compare the Second Vatican Council (1962–65) with what had preceded it. The First Vatican Council (1869–70) was called by Pope Pious IX in 1868 and was held in Rome. It was the latter period of the Ultramontanites, who pressed for centralization and the stronger influence of the Papal Curia and strongly opposed liberalism, both Catholic and Protestant. Cardinal

---

44. Ibid., 2.8 (emphasis added).
45. Ibid., 2.25.
46. Thomas F. Torrance, *God and Rationality* (London: Oxford University Press, 1971).

Manning of Westminster was a supporter of this group. John Henry Newman (1801–90), by contrast, was regarded by most people as progressive. Earlier in the nineteenth century a contrary movement had sprung up. Against the background of Enlightenment rationalism, many stressed the priority of revelation and faith and gave a minimal role to reason. On the other hand, many feared that in the wake of rationalism "faith without reason" would seem to be a matter of merely private opinion, not of knowledge. Both sides increasingly moved to adopt two extreme positions, and "the claims of faith and reason were seldom stated in a balanced way."[47]

In response to this, Pope Pius IX issued a papal encyclical in which he urged: "Although faith is above reason, no real disagreement or opposition can ever be found between them. . . . Both of them come from . . . God. They give . . . reciprocal help to each other."[48] In Vatican I *Dei Filius* discussed faith and reason further. In general the council looked back to Aquinas. It asserted that God "can be known with certainty. . . . By the natural power of human reason" from "created things" (Rom. 1:20). Nevertheless what in principle can be known by reason is to be "supernaturally revealed by God." God reveals to the eyes of faith the things that reason cannot know.[49] Any power of reason is "assisted by the Holy Spirit" and is due to supernatural grace.[50] Vatican I's chapter 4, "On Faith and Reason," distinguishes "between *how* we know, the *source* of knowledge, and *what* we know, the *object* of knowledge."[51] At one level we know the sources of knowledge by reason, but the object, who is God himself, is known only by faith. Reason and faith are thereby supposedly two different ways of knowing.

Vatican II was convened by Pope John XXIII (1958–63). About 2,600 bishops attended from various parts of the world, and Karl Rahner, Yves Congar, and Hans Küng were involved as consultants. Pope Paul VI presided over the proceedings. The council was divided into four "constitutions," of which one was *Gaudium et Spes*, which concerned the church in the modern world, mainly human dignity (1.1), the community of humankind (1.2), hu-

---

47. Francesca A. Murphy, Balázs M. Mezei, and Kenneth Oakes, *Illuminating Faith* (London: Bloomsbury, 2015), 92.

48. Pius IX, *Qui pluribus: On Faith and Reason* §6.

49. Vatican I, *Dei Filius* 2.1–4, which reflects Aquinas, *Summa Theologiae* §1 Q1 art. 1.

50. Vatican I, *Dei Filius* 3.

51. Murphy, Mezei, and Oakes, *Illuminating Faith*, 95 (emphasis original).

man activity throughout the world (1.3), and the role of the Catholic Church in the world (1.4). Part 2 deals with marriage, politics, economics, and other social problems. In §43 the church is committed to greater dialogue with the world, for "one of the greatest errors of our time is the dichotomy between the faith . . . and the practice of their [the people's] daily lives."[52]

Pope John Paul II (1920–2005) had a special interest in *Gaudium et Spes*, and in 1998 he issued the papal encyclical *Fides et ratio* ("Faith and Reason") to explicate it further. He compares faith and reason to the "two wings of a bird," which enable the human person to rise to "the contemplation of truth."[53] He quotes "know yourself" as the philosophical carving on the Oracle at Delphi and refers to Homer, Euripides, Sophocles, and even Confucius. Nevertheless, he urges, Jesus is "the Way, the Truth, and the Life," while we all share the journey of discovery with many philosophers and thinkers. Men and women, he continues, "have at their disposal an array of resources for generating greater knowledge of the truth. . . . Among these is philosophy, which is directly concerned with asking the question of life's meaning. . . . Philosophy emerges then as one of the noblest of human tasks."[54]

John Paul II cites the sense of wonder that philosophy can provide, but concludes that philosophical and rational reflection can be understood in various ways.[55] He continues: "At the same time, the Church considers philosophy to be an indispensable help for a deeper understanding of faith and for communicating the truth of the gospel to those who do not yet know it."[56] Sometimes, he admits, philosophical argument can lose its way, and end in agnosticism, atheism, and relativism. But this reduces everything to mere *opinion*. By contrast, Christians must bear witness to truth.

Chapter 1 asserts the priority and validity of the revelation of the wisdom of God. The church has received the word of God in faith (1 Thess. 2:13; 1 Cor. 2:7; 2 Cor. 4:1–2; Rom. 16:25–26). God's initiative comes from pure grace.[57] Vatican I rejected the rationalism of the times. Vatican II stressed God's

---

52. Vatican II, *Gaudium et Spes* §43; English in Austin P. Flannery (ed.), *Documents of Vatican II* (Grand Rapids: Eerdmans, 1975), 943.

53. John Paul II, *Fides et ratio* (Rome: Liberia Editrice Vaticana, 1968), introduction §1.

54. Ibid., introduction §3.

55. Ibid., introduction §4.

56. Ibid., introduction §5.

57. Ibid., chapter 1 §7.

revelation in history to bring salvation (Heb. 1:1–2; John 16:13). Revelation contains mystery, so the vision of God is fragmentary, even though through faith in Christ we may be allowed the possibility of coherence.[58] The fullness of revelation is found in Jesus of Nazareth.

In chapter 2 John Paul II declares how closely "knowledge conferred by faith and the knowledge conferred by reason" are related, citing Wisdom of Solomon 9:11 and Sirach 14:20–27.[59] Of the biblical wisdom literature he declares: "Reason is valued without being overvalued."[60] Nevertheless, "the fear of the LORD is the beginning of knowledge" (Prov. 1:7 NRSV). He then appeals to Romans 1:20, perhaps suggesting rational inferences from the creaturely world to God.[61] This verse, he says, affirms human capacity for metaphysical enquiry. But reason became corrupted by human sin; hence there is also a need for discernment (cf. 1 Cor. 1:27–28). On the other hand, he comments: "It is thinkable that a search so deeply rooted in human nature was completely vain and useless."[62]

In chapter 4 Pope John Paul considers Paul's dialogue with the Athenian philosophers in Acts 17 and cites the Eastern and Western fathers as well as medieval scholastic theology. In §§43–44 he cites Thomas Aquinas and his dialogue with Jews and Muslims. In Aquinas, he says, "faith has no fear of reason. . . . But builds upon and perfects reason."[63] After the era of Aquinas, however, a problem arose with the rise of the universities: namely a separation between faith and reason. This reached a climax in the nineteenth century. In the light of this separation chapter 5 concerns the magisterium of the church. John Paul then refers to *Gaudium et Spes* in Vatican II and the requirements for the education and training of priests.[64]

The remainder of the encyclical proceeds along the same lines. Reason and philosophy can prepare for the hearing of the word. Moral theology also needs what reason can provide. The general theme is that of the mutual support offered by faith and reason.

58. Ibid., chapter 1 §13.
59. Ibid., chapter 2 §16.
60. Ibid., chapter 2 §20.
61. Ibid., chapter 2 §22.
62. Ibid., chapter 3 §29.
63. Ibid., chapter 4 §43.
64. Ibid., chapter 5 §60.

The Faithfulness of God

We remind ourselves again of the Old Testament word *'mn*, which in the Qal verbal form means "to be reliable, put trust in, be true"; in the causative Hiphil verbal form it means "to believe, put one's trust in"; while as a noun (*'ĕmûnâ*) it means "steadiness, reliability" or in the form *'ĕmûn* means "reliable or true."[65]

One good example of insisting on maintaining this aspect of faith as faithfulness is found in the theology and exegesis of Karl Barth. In Romans 1:17, Paul writes, according to the NRSV, "the righteousness of God is revealed through faith for faith [*ek pisteōs eis pistin*]." The NIV translates this "by faith from first to last"; the NJB translates it "based on faith and addressed to faith"; while the KJV translates it "from faith to faith." Clearly the meaning of the Greek is open to debate. Barth renders it "from [his, God's] faithfulness to the faith [of humans]" in his 1919 commentary; while in the second edition of 1921 he translates it "from faithfulness unto faith."[66] He comments that faith is "from His faithfulness to us. The very God has not forgotten men; the Creator has not abandoned the creation."

Cranfield points out *seven* ways of understanding this verse.[67] N. T. Wright, however, follows Barth and argues: "In the light of 3:21-22 . . . the most natural meaning is 'from God's faithfulness to human faithfulness.'"[68] Numerous other renderings are offered. Joseph Fitzmyer regards the phrase as influenced by Psalm 84:7 and translates it as faith "from one degree to another" (cf. 2 Cor. 2:16; 3:18).[69] Tertullian regarded it as meaning "from the faith of the law to the faith of the gospel."[70] Augustine understood it to mean "from the faith of the preacher to the faith of believers."[71] Ambrosiaster

---

65. R. W. L. Moberly, "'*ĕmûn*," in *New International Dictionary of Old Testament Theology and Exegesis*, ed. Willem A. VanGemeren (Carlisle: Paternoster, 1996), 1.427-33 at 427; and F. Brown, S. R. Driver, and C. A. Briggs, *Hebrew and English Lexicon of the Old Testament* (Lafayette: Associated Publishers, 1980), 52-54.

66. Karl Barth, *The Epistle to the Romans* (London/Oxford: Oxford University Press, 1968 [orig. 1933]), 35.

67. C. E. B. Cranfield, *The Epistle to the Romans*, International Critical Commentary (Edinburgh: T&T Clark, 1975), 1.99.

68. N. T. Wright, "The Letter to the Romans," in *New Interpreter's Bible*, ed. Leander Keck (Nashville: Abingdon, 2002), 10.425.

69. Joseph A. Fitzmyer, *Romans*, Anchor Bible 33 (New York: Doubleday, 1992), 263.

70. Tertullian, *Against Marcion* 5.13 (ANF 3.39).

71. Augustine, *On the Spirit and the Letter* 11.18 (*NPNF¹* 5.90).

regarded it as meaning "from past faith to future faith"; and so on. But the interpretation taken by Wright and Barth seems to accord with Habakkuk 2:4 and other biblical passages. The only other alternative might be to follow James Dunn in understanding it to mean "trust in."[72] Trust, Dunn comments, is "the counterpart of God's faithfulness." The passage, he argues, denotes "trust in and total reliance upon God." The decisive factor for Barth remains that human "boasting" is excluded, because we are totally dependent on the reliability of God.

In Barth's view, faith was primarily a matter of trust (*fiducia*). He criticizes the Scholastics for regarding faith simply as assent, which is a more intellectualist view of faith. Faith, he said, is "trust of the heart." In Calvin's words: "We . . . only stand when by faith we recumb [rest] on God."[73] Having renounced the arrogance of the world, he continues, Christians "resign themselves to the protection of God alone." Trust in God's faithfulness and promise brings us back into the realm of "taking a stand," or speech acts. Josef Pieper writes: "To believe is equivalent to taking a position on the truth of a statement and on the actuality of the matter stated."[74] Pieper adds two relevant comments: "To say, 'I believe you, but am not quite certain' is . . . to use the word 'believe' in the improper sense"; and: "To believe always means: to believe someone and to believe something."[75] As Bultmann and Bornkamm rightly insist, faith is inseparable from to whom the faith is directed.

In Romans, as Wright and others observe, faith becomes inseparable not only from God, but also from his covenant promises. One of the great wonders of the gospel is that God, who is sovereign and free, should be willing to bind himself, to limit the range of his freedom, by promising to act in promised ways, and not in others. I add to this a second wonder: namely that in the covenant God promises his blessings in such a way that we "know where we stand," as Walther Eichrodt rightly declares.[76] The covenant is both the believer's security and the ground of the believer's assurance or even

72. James D. G. Dunn, *Romans 1-8*, Word Biblical Commentary 38 (Dallas: Word, 1988), 46.

73. John Calvin, *Calvin's Biblical Commentaries: Romans* (London: Forgotten Books, 2007 [orig. 1847]), 45.

74. Josef Pieper, *Belief and Faith* (London: Faber & Faber, 1962), 7.

75. Ibid., 15, 17.

76. Walther Eichrodt, *Theology of the Old Testament* (London: SCM, 1961), 1.38.

certainty of salvation. Thus Barth and Wright regard trust in God's covenant promises through the centuries as grounded in God's faithfulness or reliability. This fully accords with the various forms of the Hebrew word *'mn.*

Käsemann goes even further. He argues that Romans 4, along with 3:21-31, holds the key place in the epistle. Paul depicts Abraham as the prototype of faith.[77] Paul underpins the interpretation of Genesis 15:6 (Abraham "believed the LORD; and the LORD reckoned it to him as righteousness") by referring to the thesis of 3:21-31. Paul regards faith "as trust in the divine promise."[78] Philo had regarded Abraham as the prototype of faith, but in the opposite sense to Paul, namely as a person "of a devout disposition." In Paul righteousness is a gift from God, and faith does not take on "independent existence" as a religious attitude, let alone religious work, but rather as trust in God's promise.[79] Abraham "submitted without reservation to the divine promise."[80] Paul develops this in relation to God's power of resurrection (4:17), in which the point of Paul's argument is that the dead contribute nothing to their life, while the gift of faith is like God's creation from nothing.[81]

Faith, as a gift of God, leading to trust in God's promise and to the assurance of salvation and security in the covenant, remains absolutely crucial. At this point we may add two further observations. The first is Paul's notion in 1 Corinthians 12:9 that the Holy Spirit may give a special gift of faith (perhaps unusually) to some particular Christian, but not to others. By definition this cannot be the faith that brings justification to all Christians. As I argue below, this is probably the kind of faith whereby one individual encourages the whole church by his or her buoyant optimism in time of trial or difficulty.

The further notion of faith is that sometimes belief is thought of as an act of will, which some associate with John's Gospel. It is a popular myth that the notion of willing or choosing to believe is a doctrine of the Fourth Gospel. This view largely stems from John 7:17: "Anyone who resolves to do the will of God will know whether the teaching is from God" (NRSV). The KJV reads: "If any man will [*thelē*] to do his will, he shall know of the doc-

77. Ernst Käsemann, "The Faith of Abraham in Romans 4," in Käsemann's *Perspectives on Paul* (London: SCM, 1971), 79-101.

78. Ibid., 81.

79. Ibid., 82.

80. Ibid., 84.

81. Ibid., 91.

trine whether it be of God." But this passage concerns obedience or obedient action, rather than faith. Indeed, although John uses the verb "to believe" (*pisteuō*) some thirty-five times, he appears never to use the noun "faith" (*pistis*). In a detailed discussion of the will to believe, or voluntarist accounts of faith, John Hick appears to compare only Hebrews 11.[82]

Hick first directs our attention to Blaise Pascal's famous wager.[83] Pascal expressed his wager on the analogy with tossing a coin to see whether it would fall with the head or the tail uppermost. If the wager concerns the existence of God, "if you gain, you gain all; if you lose, you lose nothing." This is less innocent, however, than it sounds. Pascal's *Thoughts* make a passionate plea for theism. As Hick rightly comments: "The argument of the wager is not proposed as a normal path to belief in God; it is rather a final and desperate attempt to move the almost invincibly apathetic unbeliever."[84] It would never be used by the ordinary believer. An act of will would normally be based on knowledge.

Hick goes on to consider William James's *The Will to Believe* and F. R. Tennant's argument about the will to believe in his *Philosophical Theology* as well as in his smaller book *The Nature of Belief*.[85] The core of James's argument is that "faith is synonymous with working hypotheses. . . . [The believer's] intimate persuasion is that the odds in favour [of belief] are strong enough to warrant him acting all along on this assumption of the truth."[86] Hick, however, replies: "Such faith could only be effective if theism were already true. . . . James opens his main argument from the same premise of epistemological agnosticism as Pascal."[87] But genuine believers do not "believe" in this way. As Pieper observes: "'Believe' cannot be replaced by 'think,' 'assume,' 'consider probable,' 'suppose.'"[88] It normally involves more than James's comments about "trusting people" in everyday experience. Hick

---

82. John Hick, *Faith and Knowledge*, 2nd ed. (London: Macmillan, 1988 [orig. 1957]), 32–56 at 49.

83. Blaise Pascal, *Pensées* (London: Penguin, 1995 [orig. 1966]), 121–26.

84. Hick, *Faith and Knowledge*, 33.

85. William James, *The Will to Believe and Other Essays* (New York: Longmans, Green, 1912/Guttenberg e-books, 2009); F. R. Tennant, *Philosophical Theology* (Cambridge: Cambridge University Press, 1928), vol. 1, chap. 11.

86. James, *Will to Believe*, 95.

87. Hick, *Faith and Knowledge*, 38–39.

88. Pieper, *Faith and Belief*, 13.

declares: "This view of faith . . . is not the view of the ordinary religious believer."[89] It belongs to his wider philosophy of pragmatism. As John Lamont expresses it: "The faith of the average Christian believer is theoretically reasonable."[90]

Tennant receives the same criticism. He argues that like faith in the realm of science, faith always awaits verification. Admittedly there are arguments for this in the nature of faith in Hebrews 11, which asserts: "All of these [Old Testament believers] died in faith without having received the promises" (11:13 NRSV). But there had been sufficient continuity in the lives and experiences of Abraham and the patriarchs, Moses and Israel, and the prophets for such faith not to be groundless and unreasonable. The eschatological fulfillment would add a confirmation of what the Old Testament believers had seen only "from a distance" (11:13). Hick dismisses Tennant's arguments as "paradoxical."[91] Nevertheless he wryly concludes: "Although James and Tennant both ascribe to the human will too large and central a part in the act of faith, it would equally be a mistake to accord to it no place at all. Faith is an activity of the whole man, and as such there is a volitional side to it."[92]

I have discussed faith explicitly in relation to rational or reasonable thought and in relation to human will. I have so far said, however, not enough about the emotions. Faith may indeed touch and transform emotions, and in the biblical writings feelings are often included in language about the heart. Nevertheless my main point should be one of warning: faith does not depend on emotions or feelings. Faith may be robust and steadfast even in times of trial or of grief. People often make the point in connection with becoming a Christian, that is, becoming a believer. There is no correlation between faith and doubt, or between high and low feelings. Evangelists often say, "Don't ask whether you *feel* differently!" But this should be applied more broadly. Feelings can be a deceptive guide to faith and doubt. Again, they can be relevant; but not as a criterion of authenticity.

Throughout this chapter on faith, I have endeavored to show its many-sidedness in biblical, theological, and philosophical thought. If I have suc-

89. Hick, *Faith and Knowledge*, 42.
90. John R. T. Lamont, *Divine Faith* (Aldershot/Burlington: Ashgate, 2004), 187.
91. Hick, *Faith and Knowledge*, 51.
92. Ibid., 53.

ceeded, this corroborates my initial claim in the first chapter. Its many-sided meanings do not detract from its remaining a gift of God through the Holy Spirit, which demands total appropriation, self-involvement, and commitment, from the Christian believer.

PART III

CERTAINTY

CHAPTER 6

Differing Concepts and Contexts of Certainty

Psychological and Epistemic Certainty

Most philosophers distinguish between psychological certainty and epistemic, logical, propositional, or objective certainty. Psychological certainty is generally defined simply as a feeling or conviction of certainty, a confidence and unreserved trust in something or someone, regardless of whether there are adequate grounds for such certainty. I noted above John Locke's blistering criticisms of such certainty. Mere intensity of conviction does not guarantee the truth of the certainty that someone feels.[1] The problem about epistemic or logical certainty is that, in the words of John Frame (born 1939), "there is no universally accepted definition of this second kind of certainty"; he also doubts whether such a distinction is always clear or possible.[2]

Further distinctions may be made. Wittgenstein, for example, distinguishes between certainty in everyday life (in his words, the "language-game" of ordinary everyday language in action) and certainty in abstract philosophical discourse, which he calls "theoretical certainty." A theoretical propo-

1. John Locke, *An Essay concerning Human Understanding* (Oxford: Clarendon, 1979 [orig. 1689]), 4.19.
2. John M. Frame, with Vernon Poythress, "Certainty," in *New Dictionary of Apologetics*, ed. W. Campbell-Jack and Gavin McGrath (Leicester: IVP Academic, 2006); cf. John Frame, *Doctrine of the Knowledge of God* (Phillipsburg, NJ: P&R, 2005).

sition, he says, is an idle one: "Nothing would follow from it, and nothing could be explained by it. It would not tie in with anything in my life."[3]

Yet this distinction almost pales into insignificance compared with the huge differences determined by different contexts in life. Barron Reed points out that in the end "it is difficult to provide an uncontentious analysis of certainty. . . . One [reason] is that there are *different kinds* of certainty."[4] In other words, the *contexts* of certainty decisively shape our *concepts* of certainty. For example, what constitutes certainty in the field of law will differ drastically from certainty in the sciences, or in mathematics, or in statistics. The criteria concerning what counts as certainty will differ. At first sight a jury's verdict of "guilty" or "not guilty" may seem to be certain, until we begin to consider the possibility of an appeal, the approval of juries, and so on. We will find that the whole question of whether there is, or can be, certainty in law is highly controversial and hotly debated. In the days when only Sir Isaac Newton's laws of gravity and motion held sway in physics, certainty in the sciences, and especially physics, seemed decisive. But since perhaps Einstein and more clearly Heisenberg, matters seem to be not so simple, as soon as we leave the world of everyday.[5] Certainty in the context of Christian faith introduces a context that cannot be reduced to any other context in life. We begin to wonder whether we can speak of certainty as a meaningful concept at all.

Psychological certainty concerns simply a mental state of being supremely confident in the truth of some proposition. In special cases, it may extend to trusting a person absolutely, but this usually means trusting that this person's witness or testimony is true, which would ultimately signify unreserved belief in the truth of the propositions that he or she utters. It does not seem to go beyond subjective certainty, to ask whether such certainty or confidence can be justified. That is why John Locke is so critical of subjective or psychological certainty. It seems to ignore and undermine his notion of reasonable belief.

3. Ludwig Wittgenstein, *On Certainty* (Oxford: Blackwell, 1969), §117.

4. Barron Reed, "Certainty," in *Stanford Encyclopaedia of Philosophy*, ed. Edward N. Zalta (2011); online at plato.stanford.edu/archives/win2011/entries/certainty/.

5. Cf. Karl Heim, *The Transformation of the Scientific World View* (London: SCM, 1953); and Michael Polanyi, *Personal Knowledge: Towards a Post-Critical Philosophy* (London: Routledge & Kegan Paul, 1958); and numerous works cited below by John Polkinghorne.

The nineteenth century did indeed witness an era of what was then called "psychologism." Psychologism argues that self-observation or introspection could never establish truth beyond considering the subjective elements of human consciousness. In the first half of the century Friedrich Beneke and Jakob Fries propagated this idea. In an exaggerated form, it reflected elements of the English empiricists Locke, Berkeley, and Hume that all that a person can know is that person's ideas. In this respect all the major empiricists were idealists. John Stuart Mill then applied this to logic and mathematics. Kant could reject this approach only by postulating a transcendental realm that allowed the possibility of knowledge beyond the self. His work was followed by denials of psychologism by Hegel, Husserl, and Heidegger as well as by the neo-Kantians Hermann Cohen (1842–1918) and Paul Natorp (1854–1924). Edmund Husserl (1859–1938) was emphatic that "to psychologize the eidetic," especially in arithmetic, was monstrous.[6] (*Eidetic* differs in meaning in philosophical and psychological contexts. In philosophy, as here, it means, "pertaining to knowledge"; in psychology and in popular uses, it means "pertaining to images," especially with reference to vivid or accurate memory.) Authentic objects of knowledge, Husserl says, could not be reduced to consciousness of them.

However, virtually all expressions of absolute certainty betray an attitude of buoyant confidence, especially in biblical examples. This should not lead us to conflate psychological certainty with eidetic certainty. It merely suggests that objective, logical certainty usually also presupposes psychological certainty. Thus, to cite a biblical example, when Paul exults: "I am convinced [the perfect tense *pepeismai* indicates a present state on the basis of past events] that neither death, nor life, . . . nor anything else in all creation, will be able to separate us from the love of God in Christ Jesus" (NRSV), his "psychological certainty" is based on the rational justification or ground of everything that he has argued from Romans 4:1 to 8:17. This exactly matches N. T. Wright's exegetical comment: "The final [Greek] *gar* ('for') of this section explains the shout of triumph in terms of the settled conviction (*grounded on what Paul knows about the Messiah*, Jesus . . .) that the one true God has poured out, through this Jesus, love of the most powerful and unbreakable kind."[7]

6. Edmund Husserl, *Ideas: General Introduction to Pure Phenomenology* (London: Routledge, 2012 [orig. 1931]) §22, 40–41.

7. N. T. Wright, "The Letter to the Romans," in *New Interpreter's Bible*, ed. Leander Keck (Nashville: Abingdon, 2002), 10.614 (emphasis added).

In view of the frequency of the presupposition of psychological certainty in the absence or presence of epistemic certainty, it is, perhaps, surprising that John Frame writes: "Epistemic certainty . . . is not something sharply different from psychological certainty."[8] In Christian theology the difference may be decisive: two Christians may feel certain about what God has spoken, but in each case the grounds or epistemic warrant of their psychological certainty may be entirely different, as Locke well argued. One may be illusory; the other, genuine and grounded.

Often in the New Testament the epistemic basis of psychological certainty is relevant *action*. For example, in Matthew 9:6, Jesus says to the paralytic: "That you may know that the Son of Man has authority . . . to forgive sins. . . . Stand up . . . go to your home'" (NRSV).[9] Similarly Luke's aim "that you may know the truth [or be certain; Greek *asphaleia*] concerning the things about which you have been instructed" (Luke 1:4 NRSV) finds an epistemic basis in Luke's "investigating everything carefully from the very first" (1:3) and taking account of what was "handed on to us by those who from the beginning were eyewitnesses" (1:2). It is also relevant that Jesus "presented himself alive to them by many convincing proofs" (Acts 1:3). Luke's word for "proofs" is the Greek *tekmēria*, which Danker renders "that which causes something to be known in a convincing and decisive manner."[10] This is also the meaning in Aristotle, *Rhetoric* 1357B.4, 1402B.19, and Diodorus 17.51.3.

Hebrews and Romans have special importance as guarantors of propositional or epistemic certainty. This theme appears in Hebrews 6:13–19: "When God made a promise to Abraham, because he had no one greater by whom to swear, he swore by himself, saying, 'I will surely bless you and multiply you.' . . . An oath given as confirmation puts an end to all dispute." Hence, when God wanted to show them the situation more clearly, "he guaranteed it by an oath, so that through two unchangeable things, in which it is impossible that God would prove false, . . . we have . . . a sure and steadfast anchor of the

---

8. Frame, "Certainty," 2.

9. I discuss the christological implications of speech acts in *Thiselton on Hermeneutics: The Collected Works and New Essays of Anthony Thiselton* (Aldershot: Ashgate/Grand Rapids: Eerdmans, 2006), 75–116; *New Horizons in Hermeneutics* (Grand Rapids: Zondervan/Carlisle: Paternoster, 1992), 283–303; and "Luke, Speech-Act Theory, and Christology," in *Jesus of Nazareth: Lord and Christ*, ed. Joel B. Green and Max Turner (Grand Rapids: Eerdmans, 1994), 453–72.

10. BDAG 994.

soul" (NRSV). "The two things" are variously interpreted: some regard these as God's Word and his promise; others as God as oath taker and God as witness.

Interestingly, many modern philosophical debates claim that variations in time seriously affect certainty. What is true today may not be true tomorrow. John Locke applied this to testimony. Hence "unchangeable" here means "not subject to the contingencies of time" (Greek *pragmatōn ametathetōn*, for which Danker proposes "unalterable").[11] Still more striking, however, is that God should make promises and even confirm them by an oath. These openly place limits upon God's freedom to choose alternative actions: God commits himself irrevocably to follow a particular course of action, in this case to grant his blessing through Abraham and Christ. In everyday life, a promise to a child prohibits a choice of any more desirable action, for the sake of one's commitment to the child.[12] Philo puzzled over why God should need to swear an oath. What can an oath add, since God cannot or will not lie?[13] But God publicly observes limits to his sovereign freedom, for the sake of Israel and the church, and commits himself in a speech act for our assurance.[14]

Romans 4 likewise regards much of Paul's argument as bound up with God's promise to Abraham. God promised the "free gift" of righteousness (4:1–12), and this took the form of his promise to Abraham's heirs, so that "the promise may rest on grace and be guaranteed to all his descendants" (4:16 NRSV). Paul adds: "No distrust made him waver concerning the promise of God" (4:20); he was fully convinced that "God was able to do what he had promised" (4:21). The basis of security and certainty was most especially enshrined in the covenant, which means in Eichrodt's words, that people "know where they stand with God."[15]

---

11. BDAG 53.

12. I discussed this at length in the context of "commissive" speech acts in "The Paradigm of Biblical Promise as Trustworthy, Temporal, Transformative Speech Acts," in *The Promise of Hermeneutics*, ed. Roger Lundin, Clare Walhout, and Anthony C. Thiselton (Grand Rapids: Eerdmans, 1999), 223–39; idem, *Thiselton on Hermeneutics*, 197–31; idem, "Oath," in *New Interpreter's Dictionary of the Bible*, ed. Katharine Doob Sakenfeld (Nashville: Abingdon, 2009), 4.309–12.

13. Philo, *Sacrifices of Cain and Abel* 91–94; *Allegorical Laws* 3.203–7; cf. Thiselton, "Oath."

14. Anthony C. Thiselton, "Hebrews," in *Eerdmans Commentary on the Bible*, ed. James D. G. Dunn and John W. Rogerson (Grand Rapids: Eerdmans, 2003), 1451–82.

15. Walther Eichrodt, *Theology of the Old Testament* (London: SCM, 1961), 1.38.

Thus the confidence of psychological certainty is real for Christians, but in most cases it also presupposes a basis of epistemic or objective certainty. Some may reply that this applies only within the Christian's world. But this brings us to the next point. Concepts of certainty differ because the contexts of certainty also differ. Certainty in the context of law, economics, statistics, philosophy, social sciences, natural sciences, and Christian theology may indeed differ in meaning radically. This is not least because in each of these fields what counts as criteria of certainty may also vary.

Differing Contexts of Certainty

Some writers argue that in all practical contexts of life certainty verges on being an illusion.[16] Gerd Gigerenzer argues that our perceptual systems constantly deceive us in a mistaken search for certainty, and he illustrates this from the Necker cube and from Roger Shepard's "Turning the Tables" diagram (1990).[17] In each case the sketches are identical, but optically we find ourselves interpreting them in an illusory way. He cites how certainties of accepted authorities, which were perhaps suggested by parents and teachers, retain their grip on our perception, sometimes for life. Most worryingly, he cites the large influence of medical practitioners, in which certainty or probability is offered, because practicing clinicians rank reassurance over honest information. Patients, they claim, demand "a doctor who never errs." The World Health Organization considers uncertainty a threat to practitioners.[18] Even in the realm of probability, the sheer innumeracy of too many people makes interpretations of statistics even more uncertain. Some contexts in life are even more notoriously uncertain than others.

---

16. Thiselton, "Hebrews," 1464.

17. Gerd Gigerenzer, *Reckoning with Risk: Learning to Live with Uncertainty* (London: Penguin, 2002), chapter 2 and passim.

18. For discussion of this, see Michael Power, *Organized Uncertainty: Designing a World of Risk Management* (Oxford: Oxford University Press, 2009); Rajiv N. Rimal and Maria K. Lipinski, "Why Health Communication Is Important in Public Health," *Bulletin of the World Health Organization* 87 (2009): 247.

Uncertainty in the Law

Some writers attempt to establish the principle of legal certainty. Surely, it is argued, people must know exactly where they stand in law. A jury, for example, decides whether the accused is innocent or guilty. James R. Maxeiner, professor at the Centre in International and Comparative Law at Baltimore University, asserts: "Legal certainty is a central tenet of the rule of law as understood around the world." He quotes the Foreign Ministers of the G8 in 2007 saying: "It is imperative to adhere to the principle . . . of legal certainty."[19] He also cites the Organization for Economic Cooperation and Development (OECD) as seeking "to emphasise the necessity of establishing a rule-based society in the interests of legal certainty."[20]

Nevertheless many experts or scholars in jurisprudence cite such phenomena as the possibility of making appeals, criteria of "reasonable doubt," time limits on contracts, and corrections to verdicts deemed "unsafe." They distinguish between the *aim* of legal certainty and what *is possible in practice*. What happens when an IRA member accused of terrorism declares "I do not recognize the court"? What happens when there is a conflict between a national court and a European one, or between a state court and a federal one? Anthony D'Amato, professor at the Northwestern University School of Law, declares: "Legal certainty decreases over time. Rules and principles of law become more and more uncertain in content and application because legal systems are biased in favor of unraveling those rules and principles. . . . All we can hope for is a holding operation against uncertainty."[21]

19. James R. Maxeiner, "Some Realism about Legal Certainty in the Globalisation of the Rule of Law," *Houston Journal of International Law* 27 (2008): 27–46; and Foreign Ministers, *Declaration of the G8 Foreign Ministers on the Rule of Law* (UN Document A/RES/2/70, 2007).

20. OECD Development Assistance Committee, *Equal Access to Justice and the Rule of Law*, vol. 2 (2005); and Maxeiner, "Some Realism about Legal Certainty," 30–31.

21. Anthony D'Amato, "Faculty Paper," School of Law, Northwestern University (1983, 2010), 1, 33.

Uncertainty in Politics and Social Sciences

Claudio Cioffi-Revella (born 1951), a professor of computational social science, writes that his book is "about uncertainty in politics [and] about the defining role that the real world plays in political life."[22] Few writers, he claims, have examined this, together with the part played in politics by probability theory and game theory. He argues that political scientists, social scientists, philosophers, and epistemologists would recognize his point: "Uncertainty appears to be a characteristic of all political life."[23]

Cioffi-Revella later considers three consequences of uncertainty in politics: "Uncertainty is ubiquitous, consequential, and irradicable."[24] He also explores the emergence of uncertainty in history: in the fall of the Babylonian and Roman Empires, in numerous party realignments, in foreign regime changes, and so on. Indeed wherever there has been conflict, war, or coalition, this readily sharpens into sheer uncertainty. Social behavior, as studied in the social sciences, especially changes in the allocation of values and goals, which also reflect this uncertainty. If there were not uncertainty, it would be like "Laplacean mechanics and a lifeless pendulum."[25] The consequential aspect emerges especially in collectivities, where elections, revolutions, and conflicts play a part. The eradicable aspect, he notes, was observed first by Aristotle and then by Niccolò Machiavelli in 1512.

One of the earliest systematizers, Cioffi-Revella claims, was Thomas Hobbes in *Leviathan*, in which the sovereign, war, or anarchy could play a decisive part. In the twentieth century D. M. Fischer showed how causality relates to probabilistic prediction, not certainty, which demonstrates that uncertainty in the social sciences does not imply randomness. Elections and wars, for example, are often viewed in terms of probability. Throughout his work, Cioffi-Revella cites a massive host of authorities and authors and concludes that uncertainty is a defining principle in politics and the social sciences.[26]

22. Claudio Cioffi-Revella, *Politics and Uncertainty: Theory, Models, and Applications* (Cambridge: Cambridge University Press, 1998), xiii.
23. Ibid., 3.
24. Ibid.
25. Ibid., 5.
26. Ibid., 38.

Uncertainty in Linguistics and Linguistic Philosophy

I referred earlier to William Alston on the value at times of vagueness, who argues that "simple, clear-cut, specifications of the meanings of words" in language tend to gloss over complexities.[27] He cites in his work on vagueness the phrase "middle aged." This applies to someone of fifty; but probably wouldn't apply to people of thirty-nine, forty-one, or sixty years old. The example "we must take steps to meet this emergency" is not so much vague, as having lack of specificity. Yet in diplomacy, for example, Alston suggests, we definitely need vague terms. A diplomat may need to say, "My government will strongly oppose . . . ," without specifying what particular measures it will take. Alston insists: "The word ['vague'] can have a number of independent conditions of application."[28]

F. Waismann claims that the concept of "open texture" cannot and should not be eliminated. Words of open texture, he says, will always have a penumbra of indeterminacy.[29] Alston not only approves of Waismann's approach, but also commends the vagueness implied in metaphor. We readily speak of a "fork in the road," "a leg of the table," or the "stem of a glass." We also need synecdoche, as when we speak of "a ship opening fire."[30]

Ludwig Wittgenstein, who greatly influenced Waismann, resisted the notion of essences or "generalities" in favor of "family resemblances" or "a complicated network of similarities, overlapping, and crisscrossing."[31] He is happy with such sentences as "the ground looked roughly like this" and "concepts with blurred edges."[32] An indistinct concept, he says, is exactly what we need. He rejects a contrived ideal language and "superconcepts": "We are not striving after an ideal."[33] Examples could be multiplied. What is important is not certainty or distinctiveness, but various concrete functions and applications.[34]

27. William P. Alston, *Philosophy of Language* (Englewood Cliffs, NJ: Prentice-Hall, 1964), 84.

28. Ibid., 87.

29. F. Waismann, "Verifiability," in *Logic and Language*, ed. Anthony Flew (1st series, Oxford: Blackwell, 1952), 119–23.

30. Alston, *Philosophy of Language*, 97.

31. Ludwig Wittgenstein, *Philosophical Investigations*, 2nd ed. (Oxford: Blackwell, 1958), §§66–67.

32. Ibid., §§70–71.

33. Ibid., §98.

34. Ibid., §§108, 140, 146.

Linguistics exposes an equally great problem about certainty. John Lyons, for example, discusses the problem of being certain in his books *Theoretical Linguistics* and *Semantics*. One example from his former work concerns synonymy.[35] At first sight synonyms appear easy to define, for example, as "interchangeability in all contexts, and identity in both cognitive and emotive import."[36] But Lyons doubts whether a straightforward scale of similarity and difference is possible, not least because an almost infinite variety of contexts can be imagined. He quotes Stephen Ullmann, formerly Oxford professor of semantics, as saying: "It is almost a truism that total synonymy is an extremely rare occurrence." For example, if liberty/freedom and hide/conceal are cognitively equivalent, they are not so in emotional terms. If identity of meaning is certain, each synonym could replace the other, but this is rarely the case. Hyponymy also raises problems. The color "scarlet" at first sight is included within "red," as "tulip" is included within "flower." But even to state this is thereby to show that "red" and "flower" are themselves indeterminate words, involving lack of clarity and lack of certainty of meaning.

Among numerous examples in his work on semantics, Lyons discusses H. P. Grice's "Conversational Implicature," which rests on "a distinction between what is actually said and what is implied (but not entailed) in saying what is said."[37] In Grice's sense of the term, the concept is important and far reaching, but certainty cannot apply to all that is implied in the discourse in question. The same applies to work on the logic of presupposition. This is often unexpressed. But Austin and others demonstrated the importance of presupposition as an implied but unexpressed statement in many speech acts and speech act theory, with concrete examples.[38]

35. John Lyons, *Introduction to Theoretical Linguistics* (Cambridge: Cambridge University Press, 1968), 446–60.

36. Ibid., 448.

37. John Lyons, *Semantics* (Cambridge: Cambridge University Press, 1977), 592–606 at 592.

38. John Austin, *How to Do Things with Words* (Oxford: Clarendon, 1962), 48–54.

Uncertainty in Quantum Mechanics

This subsection serves, in effect, as an introduction to certainty and uncertainty in the world of the natural sciences. In the course of their discussions of quantum physics, John Polkinghorne and Nicholas Beale state: "The indeterminacy of the fundamental physical laws reflects a deep fact about the nature of the science of the universe. . . . Observations from measurements are probabilities."[39] They continue: "More precisely, the 'uncertainty' that seems to be at the heart of the physical world does make it clearer how true freedom and free will could emerge. This is especially true if you combine the uncertainty at very small scales with the effects of chaotic dynamics. . . . The processes that can give rise to genuine novelty have to be 'at the edge of chaos,' where order and disorder, chance and necessity, creatively interact."[40]

Polkinghorne patiently builds up a picture of physics, quantum mechanics, and the sciences as a whole, as often resting on probabilities, not certainties.[41] He traces historically how the popular or commonsense view of the sciences as objective, fixed, and certain has gradually been displaced by a less determinate view. As noted, Karl Heim demonstrates a similar program in his book *The Transformation of the Scientific World-View*.

The Transformation of the Popular Scientific Worldview

In broad outline, Heim, Polanyi, and other writers trace a similar narrative. Heim declares: "For centuries it [scientific investigation] has been accepted as self evident; namely the assumption that the world . . . is an objective world of things."[42] But in the twentieth century, he observes, two contradictory pictures emerged of light as a wave with movement and light as a particle in a location. He continues: "Either it must rest content with an

39. John Polkinghorne and Nicholas Beale, *Questions of Truth* (Louisville: Westminster John Knox Press, 2009), 42.

40. Ibid., 43.

41. John Polkinghorne, *Science and Religion in Quest of Truth* (London: SPCK, 2011), 36; and idem, *Quantum Theory* (Oxford: Oxford University Press, 2002).

42. Heim, *Transformation of the Scientific World View*, 46.

insoluble riddle, or it must . . . trespass upon the field of philosophy."[43] One turning point is Werner Heisenberg's "uncertainty principle" concerning mass and velocity in physics. Heim adds: "Human reflection in terms of the absolute object . . . has provisionally come to an end."[44] Newton's notion of a universal law of gravitation is now seen to apply only to the everyday world of "fifth-form" science, not to "higher" questions in physics. Heim then considers the work of Einstein, Heisenberg, Planck, Bohr, and others, concluding that the necessity of causal laws can be explained only in terms of probability, not of certainty.[45]

Michael Polanyi writes: "I start by rejecting the ideal of scientific detachment. . . . It is in fact disregarded by scientists. . . . It exercises a destructive influence in biology, sociology, and sociology."[46] Like Gadamer, he asserts that "a society which wants to preserve a fund of personal knowledge must submit to tradition."[47] An apprentice follows his master. He adds: "Practical wisdom is more truly embodied in action than expressed in rules of action."[48] More tellingly, he continues: "Our capacity to acquire knowledge . . . demands that we credit ourselves with much wider cognitive powers than an objectivist conception of knowledge would allow."[49] Knowledge demands participation, not just the viewpoint of a spectator.

Meanwhile John Polkinghorne writes as both an eminent physicist and Fellow of the Royal Society and also as an ordained Anglican. One of his many books considers especially modern quantum theory and its discovery since the 1920s. He begins: "What had been considered to be the arena of clear and determinate process was found to be, at its subatomic roots, cloudy and fitful in its behaviour."[50] Many interpretive issues remain unresolved. He begins with a "hint" of the quantum revolution in 1885 with Balmer, in 1897 with J. J. Thomson, and then with Max Planck, leading up to Albert Einstein at the beginning of the twentieth century. He calls these "cracks in the classi-

43. Ibid., 50.
44. Ibid., 65.
45. Ibid., 136–68.
46. Michael Polanyi, *Personal Knowledge: Towards a Post-Critical Philosophy* (London: Routledge & Kegan Paul, 1958), vii.
47. Ibid., 53.
48. Ibid., 54.
49. Ibid., 249.
50. Polkinghorne, *Quantum Theory*, preface.

cal or Newtonian world-view." Attention moved from light to atoms in 1911, with Ernest Rutherford in Manchester, and then with the Danish physicist Niels Bohr in 1913, with the "Bohr atom."

Quantum theory entered the scene around 1925–26, with Heisenberg in Germany. His earliest work was known as matrix mechanics and was developed as wave mechanics by Austrian physicist Erwin Schrödinger. Heisenberg and Schrödinger made faster progress, when their work was further developed by Max Born in Göttingen and Paul Dirac, Polkinghorne's supervisor, in Cambridge. In 1930 Dirac published *Principles of Quantum Mechanics*, which Polkinghorne calls "one of the intellectual classics of the twentieth century."[51] He demonstrated that an electron had no single position, but "states of 'here' and 'there.'" A theoretically indivisible electron could simultaneously appear in two places. Polkinghorne continues: "It was Max Born at Göttingen who first clearly emphasised the *probabilistic* character of quantum theory."[52] For this Born received the Nobel Prize in 1954. Polkinghorne repeats the conclusion expressed in his preface: "Classical physics describes a world that is clear and determinate. Quantum physics describes a world that is cloudy and fitful."[53]

Admittedly classical physics dealt also with probabilities. Tossing a coin results on average in 50% for heads and 50% for tails. But "laws for combining probabilities are different in quantum theory."[54] Heisenberg's uncertainty principle applies to time and energy, as well as to positions and movement.[55] Polkinghorne then compares solid matter and crystals, in which new properties of atoms can be revealed, including properties "intermediate between those of individual atoms and values of free moving particles."[56] There follows an evaluation of Dirac's "quantum field theory," in which the field "has an infinite number of degrees of freedom."[57] New mathematical techniques are needed for distinguishing between particle theory and field theory. Polkinghorne concludes: "The study of quantum physics teaches one . . . that the

51. Ibid., 20.
52. Ibid., 25 (emphasis added).
53. Ibid., 26.
54. Ibid., 41.
55. Ibid., 58.
56. Ibid., 63.
57. Ibid., 73.

world is full of surprises. . . . Quantum theory encourages us to keep fluid our conception of what is reasonable; it also encourages us to recognise that there is no universal epistemology. . . . Insisting on a naïvely objective account of electrons can only lead to failure."[58] Philosophers, he says, have not always adequately taken into account the implications of these holistic aspects of quantum theory.[59]

In *Questions of Truth*, Polkinghorne declares: "The 'uncertainty' that seems to be at the heart of the physical world does make it clearer how true freedom and free will could emerge."[60] This became clearer in the light of quantum theory. In his book *Science and Religion* he observes: "There is no question that quantum physics has turned out to be probabilistic."[61] There is, he says, an "irreducible degree of openness present in natural processes."[62] In *The Polkinghorne Reader*, he considers the different kinds of understanding the world in physics, biology, and more distinctively in "human" values and admits: "We understand very little of how these different levels relate to each other."[63]

Pannenberg also describes "*the whole system of physics as a system of hypotheses.*"[64] He further notes how Thomas Kuhn's new paradigms give attention to a consensus among scientists, which may take us back, once again, to uncertainty in the social sciences and politics. This remains the case, even if we grant that Kuhn's suggestions may well be a little exaggerated. Pannenberg and Gadamer both add further implications to any notion of certainty in the sciences by stressing the need for hermeneutical understanding with its contextual, linguistic, and historical dimensions.

In his book *The Way the World Is*, Polkinghorne remarks (once again): "In a remarkable interplay of contingent chance (to get things going) and lawful necessity (to keep them going) there had begun a process by which

---

58. Ibid., 87.
59. Ibid., 90.
60. Ibid., 43.
61. Polkinghorne, *Science and Religion in Quest of Truth*, 36.
62. Ibid., 37.
63. Thomas Jay Oord (ed.), *The Polkinghorne Reader: Science, Faith, and the Search for Meaning* (London: SPCK/Templeton, 2010), 25.
64. Wolfhart Pannenberg, *Theology and the Philosophy of Science* (Philadelphia: Westminster, 1976), 56 (emphasis original).

systems of ever-increasing complexity would evolve."[65] There needs to be "an interplay between chance and necessity."[66] It would take us into a separate area to note that he thinks that this amounts to a rehabilitation of the argument from design to the existence of God. We need, he says, a world as big and complex as it is in order to allow human life to emerge within it. This simply shows that conclusions about certainty and uncertainty in the sciences in no way undermine Christian belief or faith.

65. John Polkinghorne, *The Way the World Is* (London: SPCK/Triangle, 1983), 8.
66. Ibid., 11.

CHAPTER 7

Three Approaches to Certainty

Pseudocertainty in Analytical Statements

Many statements appear to be beyond doubt in everyday life, but turn out to be simply what philosophers since Kant call analytical statements. The first step toward identifying the distinctive logic of such statements was anticipated by Gottfried Leibniz (1646–1716) the logician, mathematician, and philosopher. John Locke (1632–1704) may have implied the notion of such statements, and David Hume (1711–76) the empiricist went further than his predecessors.

It was, however, Immanuel Kant (1724–1804), who formally identified analytical statements (which he called "analytical judgments") at the beginning of his *Critique of Pure Reason* (1781). In his introduction he writes that judgments about the relations between a subject and predicate may be of two kinds: "Either the predicate B belongs to the subject A as something contained (though covertly) in the concept A; or B lies outside the sphere of the concept A, though somehow connected with it."[1] He calls the first judgment or statement "analytical"; and the second, "synthetical." He comments: "Our knowledge is in no way extended by an analytical judgment." He then cites as an example "a body has extension and gravity." If this was inherent or implied by our understanding of "body" this added no new knowledge

---

1. Immanuel Kant, *Critique of Pure Reason*, 2nd ed. (New York: Macmillan, 1922 [orig. 1896]), 1.

beyond what we already knew. It merely ordered our understanding in a better way.

Leibniz shows that the logic of such statements makes their contradiction impossible. Hence in this sense they seem indubitable and perhaps certain. Kant calls such statements "explicative" because they make explicit what is merely implied in the concept. He calls synthetical judgments "ampliative"; they add knowledge from outside. The well-worn example of an analytical statement in philosophy is "bachelors are unmarried." It is true by logical necessity, not by contingent inference. Kant tends to associate analytical statements with a priori knowledge: that is, knowledge prior to human experience or observation. Empirical evidence may confirm or disconfirm the statements, whereas analytical statements cannot be contradicted. Hume distinguishes analytical statements that are true by logical necessity from synthetic statements that needed to be confirmed by contingent truths.

In the history of philosophy after Kant, many defined an analytical statement as one that states a formal or logical truth. It is true by logical necessity. Does this mean, in the end, that it is true simply by definition? Gottlob Frege (1848–1925), founder of modern mathematical logic, extends Kant's notion of analytical judgments. Whereas Kant restricts "analytical" to such a priori propositions as "every triangle has three sides," Frege extends the term to include some examples of synthetic propositions. For example, in "7 + 5 = 12," "equal to 12" is not contained in the concept "7 + 5"; but Frege argues that it is part of its "formal" definition. Indeed he includes statements that are true by definition among analytical propositions, that is, those whose proof lay only in "general laws and definitions," such as "no bachelor is married." Those propositions thus amount to what Waismann calls logical tautologies. Others reject this idea on the basis that the proposition would then become only about meanings, not about truths or reality at all. In 1947 Rudolf Carnap distinguished "synthetic" truth from those statements that claim to be true merely because "the semantic rules of the system suffice for establishing its truth."[2]

Following Carnap, A. J. Ayer (1910–89), the leading British exponent of logical positivism, argues that there are only two kinds of "true" statements. Either they must be empirically verified (or verifiable in principle),

2. Rudolf Carnap, *Meaning and Necessity: A Study in Semantics and Modal Logic*, 2nd ed. (Chicago: University of Chicago Press, 1947), 2.17.

or else they must be analytical statements, that is, statements that derive their truth from formal or "internal" logical validity. All other propositions, for example, in ethics, art or religion, are "nonsense" or "devoid of literal significance."[3] From the point of view of our subject, Ayer writes: "In saying that the certainty of a priori propositions depends upon the fact that they are tautologies, I use the word 'tautology' in such a way that a proposition can be said to be a tautology if it is analytic . . . , true solely in virtue of the meaning of its constituent symbols."[4] Further examples include "frozen water is ice," "two halves make up a whole," or, in a more extended fashion, "water boils at 100° C," for 100° C is contained in "water boils."

The most prominent philosopher to reject the analytic/synthetic distinction was the American philosopher Willard van Orman Quine (1908–2000), also an empiricist or logical positivist. He concedes that some propositions rely on nothing but meaning and logic for their supposed truth value, but insists that no philosopher has given a definitive criterion concerning the difference between analytical and synthetic statements.[5] This is partly because, for example, statements about frozen water and ice, or water boiling at 100° C, derive their meaning from a wide body of knowledge, not from mere definition alone. Many analytical statements turn out to be only about language and definition. Thus Quine, for example, is skeptical about statements concerning the interchangeability of synonyms except as a purely intralinguistic or formal exercise.

However, numerous thinkers dissent from Quine. Hilary Putnam (1926–2016), a well-known critic of logical positivism and a foremost American philosopher and mathematician, attacked Quine's objections. Paul Grice (1913–88), an eminent philosopher on meaning, semantics, and "implicature," and P. F. Strawson (1919–2006), Oxford philosopher and logician, attacked Quine's *Two Dogmas of Empiricism*. Three further eminent philosophers and linguists, Jerrold Katz (1932–2002), Scott Soames (born 1946), and Saul Kripke (born 1940), also dissent from Quine's approach.

3. A. J. Ayer, *Language, Truth, and Logic* (London: Penguin, 1971 [1st ed. 1936; 2nd ed. 1946]), 7–8, 21–22, 48–49.

4. Ibid., 21.

5. Willard van Orman Quine, "Two Dogmas of Empiricism," in Quine's *From a Logical Point of View* (Cambridge: Harvard University Press, 1953), 20–46; first published in *Philosopher's Review* 60 (1951): 20–43.

What does all this imply for our main subject? At first sight analytical propositions seem to qualify as statements of certainty. The *Catholic Encyclopaedia* defines "certitude" as "such assent to the truth of a proposition as excludes all real doubt." On this basis such propositions as "every triangle has three sides" or "all bachelors are unmarried" seem to fit the definition of certitude. But a moment's reflection suggests that such certainty would be a purely logical or linguistic affair, having no currency in life or the everyday world. Wittgenstein describes such language as "idle," in the sense of having no application in everyday life. He suggests several analogies: "It is as if someone were to buy several copies of the morning paper to assure himself that what it said was true"; or like someone's saying, "'But I know how tall I am!,' and laying his hand on top of his head to prove it."[6] Such certainty would be illusory, because it has no role in life.

Looking backward at some of his purely logical propositions in the *Tractatus*, Wittgenstein remarked: "The language-game in which they are to be applied is missing."[7] He continues: "A *picture* held us captive. . . . Is the word ever actually used in this way . . . in its original home [i.e., in its everyday use]?"[8] The picture was one of the "crystalline purity" of formal logic: it looked perfect and indubitable, but was remote from life. The picture suggested by analytical propositions appears to hold out absolute truth and certainty, but is ultimately empty and illusory.

Wittgenstein's Provisional, Perhaps Ambiguous, Book *On Certainty*

Wittgenstein's book *On Certainty* was first published in 1969, eighteen years after his death. It was written at four different periods, all in the form of a first draft.[9] Hence controversial interpretations and possible ambiguity should not surprise us. The background to the entire discussion is G. E. Moore (1873–1958), "A Defence of Common Sense." Moore was a commonsense Yorkshireman (although professor at Cambridge). For example, when F. H.

6. Ludwig Wittgenstein, *Philosophical Investigations*, 2nd ed. (Oxford: Blackwell, 1958), §§265, 279.
7. Ibid., §96.
8. Ibid., §§115–116.
9. Ludwig Wittgenstein, *On Certainty* (Oxford: Blackwell, 1969), vi.

Bradley claims that "time is unreal," Moore replies: "Why, then, do we not take lunch *before* breakfast?" To prove the existence of the external world, Moore simply holds up his hands, saying: "There is one hand" and "here is another"; "I know this to be true."[10] Even Hume was not skeptical about such things. Wittgenstein's book is largely a response to Moore, but it must be remembered that it is unfinished work, and A. C. Grayling rightly calls it "provisional." The main contours, however, are clear: it aims to be a refutation of skepticism, and it attempts a justification of knowledge. The themes of doubt, certainty, and knowledge remain closely related.

Wittgenstein is at one with Moore in his attack on skepticism. But he is exploring whether a better "proof" or argument for this can be offered than Moore's. Statements such as "here is a hand" or "the earth has existed for a long time" seem self-evident, but there is no context in life in which it would be legitimate to doubt such statements. We can claim knowledge, Wittgenstein seems to say, only where doubt is also conceivable. Otherwise it might seem to be the pseudocertainty of logical or analytical propositions. He takes as an example "I know that I am a human being." But what would it be to consider the negative of this? "Can I doubt it? Grounds for *doubt* are lacking!"[11] Skepticism in this case would be idle and unmotivated, lacking any basis. Wittgenstein introduces a distinction between "knowing" and "being certain" ("'I am certain' could replace 'I know' in every piece of testimony," for example, in a law court, where it is a situation in everyday life).[12] Nevertheless Wittgenstein suggests that "I thought I knew" can be "no guarantee of knowledge. . . . Saying 'you know it' doesn't make it so."[13] Moore's "I know" is therefore not only idle, but out of place.

There are situations in which "I know" or "I am certain" could be mistaken, for example, in seeing a book, but with visual impairment.[14] On the other hand, knowing counts as knowledge when others can see how you reached such knowledge. Wittgenstein writes: "If the other person is ac-

---

10. G. E. Moore, "A Defence of Common Sense," in *Philosophical Papers* (London: Allen & Unwin, 1959), 32–35; and idem, "Proof of My External World," in Moore's *Selected Writings* (London: Routledge, 1993), 147–70.

11. Wittgenstein, *On Certainty* §4.

12. Ibid., §8.

13. Ibid., §§12, 15.

14. Ibid., §17.

quainted with the language-game, he would admit that I know."[15] In Moore's thought, "I thought I knew" is overlooked.[16]

Much depends, in Wittgenstein's judgment, on the frame of reference within which doubt or knowledge occurs: "The truth of certain empirical propositions belongs to our frame of reference. The truths which Moore says he *knows*, are such as, roughly speaking, *all* of us know. . . . All testing, all confirmation and disconfirmation of a hypothesis takes place already *within a system*."[17] Wittgenstein adds that "it is the *inherited background* against which I distinguish between true and false."[18] Foundations are what make the system possible, and there seems to be a match between what Wittgenstein calls "inherited background" and what the Christian church usually calls "tradition."

This also impinges on doubt. Wittgenstein writes: "If you tried to doubt *everything*, you would not get as far as doubting anything. The game of doubting itself *presupposes* certainty."[19] Similarly "doubts form a system."[20] He adds: "The child learns to believe a host of things, i.e., it learns to act according to these beliefs. Bit by bit these form a system of what is believed, and in that system some things stand unshakeably fast, and some are more or less liable to shift. What stands fast . . . is . . . held fast by what lies around it."[21] He continues: "The child learns by believing the adult. Doubt comes *after* belief."[22] Behavior and action, in the end, constitute the criteria of genuine belief and knowledge: "Justifying the evidence comes to an end. . . . It is our *acting*, which lies at the bottom of the language-game," that is, not a further set of propositions.[23] This approach and conviction reflects the *Philosophical Investigations*. He compares the role of the proposition "it is written" (cf. Matt. 4:4).[24] Hence he adds: "What I hold fast to is not *one* but a *nest* of propositions."[25]

---

15. Ibid., §18.
16. Ibid., §21.
17. Ibid., §§83, 100, 105 (emphasis added).
18. Ibid., §94 (emphasis added).
19. Ibid., §115 (emphasis added).
20. Ibid., §126.
21. Ibid., §144.
22. Ibid., §160 (emphasis original).
23. Ibid., §204 (emphasis original).
24. Ibid., §216.
25. Ibid., §225 (emphasis added).

I must clarify the significance and seriousness of Wittgenstein's term "language-game," which he used in *Philosophical Investigations*, *Zettel*, and elsewhere. "Game" seems to come from the formalists, who viewed arithmetic on the analogy of a game played with mathematical symbols. At one point he says: "I shall call the whole, consisting of language and the actions into which it is woven, the 'language-game.'"[26] He declares: "The term 'language-*game*' is meant to bring into prominence the fact that the *speaking* of language is part of *an activity*, or a form of *life*."[27] But he also adds: "I . . . have nowhere said what the essence of a language-game . . . is," because he is deeply suspicious of all generalities, essences, or "super-concepts."[28] In *Zettel* he speaks of "a great field of language-games."[29]

To return to certainty, Wittgenstein concedes that it seems "strange" that when he is "certain" about the use and meaning of words, he can give "no grounds" for this, but "none is as certain as the very thing they were supposed to be the grounds for."[30] We cannot investigate the "hinges" on the door on which *our beliefs turn*.[31] Certainty is sometimes "already *presupposed* in the language-game . . . something must be taught as a foundation."[32]

Wittgenstein posited two important arguments against skepticism. The first is his notion of the "hinge" proposition, on which other propositions turn. The second is that "I know" in Moore is often completely divorced from everyday life, but relies on a distinctively philosophical and abstract context. Such is also the picture offered of *On Certainty* by Duncan Pritchard in the *Oxford Handbook to Wittgenstein*.[33] We do not notice, Wittgenstein argues, "how very specialized the use of 'I knew' is."[34] Nor can we claim "I know" straight off; knowledge requires learning from others over a period of time. Pritchard may seem to complicate Wittgenstein further! But his contribution includes the exposure of how ambiguous *On Certainty* might be on some points.

---

26. Wittgenstein, *Philosophical Investigations* §7.
27. Ibid., §23 (emphasis original).
28. Ibid., §65.
29. Ludwig Wittgenstein, *Zettel* (Oxford: Blackwell, 1967), §43.
30. Wittgenstein, *On Certainty* §307.
31. Ibid., §343.
32. Ibid., §§446, 449 (emphasis added).
33. Duncan Pritchard, "Wittgenstein on Scepticism," in *Oxford Handbook to Wittgenstein*, ed. M. McGinn (Oxford: Oxford University Press, 2011), 523–49 at 523–24.
34. Wittgenstein, *On Certainty* §11.

Grice, among others, Pritchard reminds us, also shows how important conversations with others may be. Hence a bare assertion of certainty, as in Moore, amounts only to psychological certainty or subjective certainty, not epistemic certainty. Moreover, just as knowledge or certainty requires a supporting basis, so do doubts about it. Wittgenstein writes: "Doesn't one need grounds for doubt? Wherever I look, I find no ground for doubting that!"[35] Ultimately, "testing" occurs within a "nest of propositions," or system of beliefs. Pritchard helpfully distinguishes the "indubitability" of a proposition in Descartes from what this is in Wittgenstein. In Descartes the term signifies "it cannot be doubted." But in Wittgenstein it appears to mean that rational grounds for doubt cannot be offered. Hence, Pritchard argues, Wittgenstein does not seem to fulfill the usual foundationalist rubric for basic belief. Indeed he may perhaps be ambiguous about the when and whether reasons for believing may in the end be groundless, for at one point he declares: "The difficulty is to realize the groundlessness of our believing."[36]

Wittgenstein's appeal to hinge propositions as certain may seem to reflect a groundless faith, Pritchard comments. But would this not lead to the skepticism that Wittgenstein attacks? He declares that our questions and doubts "depend on the fact that some propositions are exempt from doubt . . . like hinges on which those turn. . . . Certain things are *indeed* not doubted."[37] The hinge-proposition notion, Pritchard suggests, is not only central; it contributes to our "epistemic angst." If we doubt hinge propositions, a question mark hangs over the whole system or framework within which our propositions receive their currency. Wittgenstein adds: "I really want to say that a language-game is only possible if one trusts something."[38] He urges constantly the illegitimacy of the philosophical context in which both skepticism and G. E. Moore are working. The possible ambiguity arises concerning what kind of propositions and context he wants to substitute for them. He traveled some mileage along a positive road, but then it sometimes seems to be in danger of beginning a circular path back again. This may be because so often his method is to stimulate debate by asking questions rather

35. Ibid., §§122–23.
36. Ibid., §166.
37. Ibid., §§341–42.
38. Ibid., §509.

than answering them. We must also remember that his work is unfinished and was never authorized for publication.

Some suggest that one way forward is to understand hinge propositions as working only within certain contexts. Would this perhaps suggest some commonality at certain points with Plantinga and Wolterstorff and Reformed epistemology? A contextual interpretation is arguable, but not decisively clear. There does seem to be more than a hint that propositions of certainty have to be presupposed rather than functioning as a subsequent supporting argument. Less convincing are those interpreters who regard *On Certainty* as a largely pragmatic argument, even if Wittgenstein's appeal to others and the community may suggest hints in this direction. A pragmatic understanding seems to trivialize much of Wittgenstein's work.

If we return to the previous point that hinge propositions may be presupposed, it is noteworthy that Hans-Johann Glock declares: "By far Wittgenstein's most important claim about hinge propositions is that they can be neither justified nor doubted, since their certainty is presupposed in all judging."[39] In *On Certainty* §494 Wittgenstein declares: "I cannot doubt this proposition without giving up all judgment." In §614 he says: "If I were contradicted on all sides . . . in that case the foundation of all judging would be taken away from me."

Because these are not finished notes, it is hazardous to reach firm conclusions about them. The host of interpreters who offer differing interpretations should perhaps be an adequate warning about doing this. A. J. Ayer's critique is especially complex and questionable.[40] But many more might be cited. From a Christian perspective, no secular philosopher, including Wittgenstein, has clearly established what it is to be certain, only the questions that must be asked en route. For the Christian, this is hardly surprising, because all human beings are creaturely, finite, and fallible. We may look to the Christian philosophy of Plantinga and Wolterstorff for a more solid way forward. At very least, however, Wittgenstein opposed skepticism, clarified the illusory nature of some supposed certainties, and, like Plantinga, saw

39. Hans-Johann Glock, "Certainty," in Glock's *A Wittgenstein Dictionary* (Oxford: Blackwell, 1996), 76–81 at 79 (citing *On Certainty* §§308, 494, 614).

40. A. J. Ayer, "Wittgenstein on Certainty," in *Royal Institute of Philosophy Lectures: 1972/73*, ed. Godfrey Verey (London: Macmillan, 1974), 226–45.

support for knowledge not in single propositions, but in a system or nest of propositions, which function for action in life.

Reformed Epistemology

Alvin Plantinga (born 1932) together with Nicolas Wolterstorff (born 1932) and William Alston (1921–2009) are the three major founders of Reformed epistemology. The approach is so named because Plantinga and Wolterstorff taught at Calvin College in Grand Rapids before their respective moves to the University of Notre Dame (Plantinga in 1982) and Yale University (Wolterstorff in 1989) and stood in the Calvinist and Christian Reformed tradition. Alston, however, was Episcopalian and had proposed the term "Episcopalian epistemology." They have shared their stance with many Roman Catholics and other Christians. Plantinga writes that their "principal claim is that *belief in God* (i.e., as Creator, Provider, all-knowing, almighty, and good) can be 'properly basic.'"[41] His equally prominent claim is that we should regard Christian belief as rational, reasonable, and justified. This does not depend, however, on evidential inferences. This would lead us too far in the direction of classical foundationalism.

As in Wittgenstein, certainty or justification does not depend on isolated propositions offering inferences on which to base justified belief. Likewise Reformed epistemology does not draw certainty from isolated propositions, from which inferences are made. Plantinga is not replicating the path of Descartes, Locke, or Hume. Rather he is seeking a "warrant" that will separate knowledge from mere opinion or belief. Ultimately, like Barth, he regards this as depending on the entire Christian belief system as revealed by God. But this is emphatically *not* fideism. The basis for belief is rational, as John Calvin and Thomas Aquinas maintained. Arguments often offered in apologetics and philosophy of religion are not regarded as irrelevant. But neither are they primarily a way of arriving at belief or knowledge. They are merely possible counterreplies to "defeaters," which might otherwise cause us to revise what we had thought of as a belief or as

---

41. Alvin Plantinga, "Reformed Epistemology," in *A Companion to Philosophy of Religion*, ed. Philip L. Quinn and Charles Taliaferro (Oxford: Blackwell, 1999), 383–89 at 383.

knowledge. They serve as a posteriori confirmation (or disconfirmation if they are unsuccessful).

Plantinga and Wolterstorff jointly published *Faith and Rationality* in 1984, and Plantinga published *Warrant: The Current Debate* in 1993.[42] The book on warrant then became the first of three, followed by *Warrant and Proper Function* in 1994 and the *Warranted Christian Belief* in 2000.[43] In 2014 he published *Knowledge and Christian Belief* to help those readers who found *Warranted Christian Belief* too technical and complex and aiming to cover the same ground in "a shorter and . . . more user-friendly version."[44]

Plantinga begins *Knowledge and Christian Belief* with a comment on the popular view that Christian belief has no rational justification. He quotes Richard Dawkins as saying: "The irrationality of religion is a by-product of a particular built-in irrationality mechanism in the brain."[45] This, he claims, represents the disease of today. This approach is widely debated, most notably in Rupert Sheldrake's book *The Science Delusion*.[46] Dawkins's approach, Plantinga argues, follows the logical positivists of the mid-twentieth century. I digress for a moment to explore a little further the Dawkins-Sheldrake debate, before returning to Plantinga.

Richard Dawkins (born 1941) is a militant atheist, who sometimes writes more like a scientific journalist than a scientist. But he is a Fellow of the Royal Society and Fellow of New College, Oxford, and has undertaken research on phenotypes. He has written *The Blind Watchmaker* and *The Selfish Gene*. He is what many regard as an old-fashioned materialist, and he develops this worldview into polemical atheism. Rupert Sheldrake (born 1942) is a Fellow of Clare College, Cambridge, and writes on cell biology and biochemistry. In his book *The Science Delusion*, he challenges whether Dawkins's worldview genuinely springs from scientific method. From the start, he attacks the notion that human beings, animals, and even plants are all "genuinely

---

42. Alvin Plantinga and Nicholas Wolterstorff, *Faith and Rationality: Reason and Belief in God* (Notre Dame: University of Notre Dame Press, 1984); and Alvin Plantinga, *Warrant: The Current Debate* (New York: Oxford University Press, 1993).

43. Alvin Plantinga, *Warrant and Proper Function* (New York: Oxford University Press, 1994); and idem, *Warranted Christian Belief* (New York: Oxford University Press, 2000).

44. Alvin Plantinga, *Knowledge and Christian Belief* (Grand Rapids: Eerdmans, 2014).

45. Richard Dawkins, *The God Delusion* (London: Bantam, 2006), 184; cf. Plantinga, *Knowledge and Christian Belief*, vii.

46. Rupert Sheldrake, *The Science Delusion* (London: Hodder & Stoughton, 2012).

programmed machines in a mechanical universe."[47] He queries whether a mechanistic model of the universe is in fact demanded by science.[48] Indeed he argues that the model of a machine is simply a metaphor, which few could take seriously in its broadest application to human beings, art, and so forth.[49] Among other core claims, he contests that all matter is unconscious, that the laws of nature are fixed and causative, and that nature is purposeless. We have seen from the debates of Heim, Polkinghorne, and Lakatos among others that there is a distinctly dated look to Dawkins's conception of the sciences. As I noted, Plantinga associates his view with mid-twentieth century logical positivism.

To return to Plantinga, he implies that, according to Dawkins, Christian belief lacks warrant, as Karl Marx and Sigmund Freud claimed. In his preface, Plantinga then outlines his agenda chapter by chapter. In chapter 1 he shows how Kant regarded reason simply as ordering or conditioning how we see things, as if, he suggests, we could see everything through "rose colored glasses: the world looks that way, not because it really is rose colored, but because of the glasses I'm wearing."[50] In other words, he continues, we are at home in a world of appearance, in part because we ourselves have constituted it. It follows from this that human reason cannot apprehend God.

In his second chapter Plantinga considers de jure objections to religious belief. According to such objections, people may argue (1) that belief is unjustified; (2) that beliefs cannot survive in the face of the pluralism of various beliefs; (3) that religious claims are arrogant; and/or (4) that belief is inferential. Then, one by one, he responds to these objections, which in a different context he later calls "defeaters." What lies behind these objections is the false expectation of propositional evidence and inference; for example, the success of the three main arguments for the existence of God. These arguments have their uses, but they are not decisive. They do not constitute evidence for *everything* that the Christian theist believes. What Plantinga calls "basic beliefs" cannot be accepted on the evidential basis of other beliefs, that is, by drawing inferences from them. The believer is justified in accepting basic beliefs in their noninferential role.

47. Ibid., 54.
48. Ibid., 28–29.
49. Ibid., 55.
50. Plantinga, *Knowledge and Christian Belief*, 2.

John Locke, Plantinga continues, saw that inferences from other propositions were less certain, or gave belief less justification, than self-evident beliefs. For example, these might be beliefs about our own experience (e.g., "I am in pain") or "incorrigible" beliefs of a logical mind (e.g., "nothing can be both red and green all over," or "$2 + 2 = 4$"). He regarded these as basic beliefs.[51]

Nevertheless, Plantinga points out: "Christian beliefs aren't just self-evident, like $2 + 1 = 3$, and neither, of course, are they just about one's own mental states. Therefore, according to the classical foundationalist, Christian beliefs must be accepted on the basis of arguments . . . on the evidential basis of *other* propositions."[52] The term "foundationalism" is often used in American philosophy and theology, but much less frequently in Britain and in Europe. Most philosophers agree that Descartes and Locke are to be called foundationalist. Paul Moser seems to provide a succinct definition: "Knowledge and epistemic . . . justification have a two-tier structure."[53] The two tiers are nonfoundational beliefs that we may hold, and noninferential or foundational knowledge and justification on which these beliefs rest. In Descartes these "foundational beliefs guarantee certainty of the non-foundational beliefs they support."[54] Plantinga gives, perhaps, his clearest definition in *Warranted Christian Belief*: "The crucial notion is that of believing one proposition on the evidential basis of others."[55] The alternative to an "evidential basis" is a "basic" proposition: "I simply see that they are true and accept them. I accept many propositions in this way: that there is snow in my backyard, for example."[56] He continues: "The propositions that I accept in this basic way are the foundations of my structure of beliefs—my 'noetic structure.'"

Plantinga next acknowledges that belief counts as "rational" in given circumstances. The important thing is to avoid any cognitive malfunctioning and to seek an adequate warrant for justified belief. We need to avoid, for

---

51. Ibid., 15.

52. Ibid., 16 (emphasis added).

53. Paul K. Moser, "Foundationalism," in *The Cambridge Dictionary of Philosophy*, ed. Robert Audi (Cambridge: Cambridge University Press, 1995), 276–78 at 276.

54. Ibid., 277.

55. Plantinga, *Warranted Christian Belief*, 82.

56. Ibid., 83.

example, what Freud would call a wish fulfillment. He comments: "A belief has *warrant* only if it is produced by cognitive faculties that are *functioning properly*, subject to no disorder or dysfunction."[57]

The next topic concerns warranted belief in God. Here Plantinga builds on the groundwork of Thomas Aquinas and John Calvin. (He calls this "the A/C model.") According to Aquinas, he says, "to know in a general and confused way that God exists is implanted in us by nature."[58] Calvin asserts exactly the same thing on the basis of Romans 1:18–20.[59] Calvin adds that we cannot go beyond this "confused" knowledge of God, "except through the gospel." He further expounds this comment in the *Institutes*.[60] Plantinga understands these comments to be referring to a kind of faculty or cognitive mechanism (like sight or hearing), which Calvin calls *sensus divinitatis*. We do not have to decide about it before acquiring it, although it often does acquire a certain growth or maturity to discern what is implanted within. This fits well with his notion of basic beliefs: they are not arrived at by decision or inference, but in the more immediate way.[61] Thus basic belief is "properly basic with respect to warrant. . . . *Theistic belief can be properly basic with respect to justification*."[62] Yet, like Aquinas and Calvin, Plantinga admits that this faculty can be diseased or disabled in various cases. He compares as examples being blind, deaf, or insane. The contentions of Freud and Marx will be true in some or many cases, but not in all cases. Paul, for example, he says, regards unbelief as a result of dysfunction. (The Hebrew words for sin confirm this.) Plantinga provides a longer discussion in *Warranted Christian Belief* of rationality, Christian belief, and warrant.[63]

Plantinga's next section introduces and discusses faith. As I argue throughout this book, he acknowledges first of all that "the term 'faith,' like

---

57. Plantinga, *Knowledge and Christian Belief*, 27 (emphasis original).

58. Thomas Aquinas, *Summa Theologiae* (Oxford: Blackfriars, 1963), §1 Q2 art. 1; cf. Aquinas, *Summa Contra Gentiles* (New York: Hangover House, 1955–57), 3.38, where he adds that implanted knowledge "is in almost all men"; and Plantinga, *Knowledge and Christian Belief*, 32.

59. John Calvin, *Calvin's Biblical Commentaries: Romans* (London: Forgotten Books, 2007 [orig. 1847]), 45–49.

60. John Calvin, *Institutes of the Christian Religion*, ed. Henry Beveridge (London: James Clarke, 1957), 1.3.1.

61. Plantinga, *Knowledge and Christian Belief*, 36–37.

62. Ibid., 37 (emphasis original).

63. Plantinga, *Warranted Christian Belief*, 108–34, 135–66, 167–356, respectively.

nearly any useful philosophical term, is used *variously, in a number of different but analogically connected senses.*"[64] He outlines most of the uses discussed above. In this context, in Calvin's words, faith is "a firm and certain knowledge of God's benevolence towards us," that is, a firm and certain knowledge that many share.[65] According to Thomas Aquinas, John Calvin, and Jonathan Edwards, God initiated such faith or certain knowledge through his Holy Spirit and Scripture. But the acquisition and growth of genuine faith is often a long process, especially entailing historical investigation of Scripture and prayer through the Holy Spirit. Thus Plantinga quotes Calvin to the effect that often "in the believing mind *certainty is mixed with doubt. . . .* We are troubled on all sides by the agitation of unbelief."[66] Plantinga further comments that degrees of belief will vary and that belief "typically varies from time to time."[67] His conclusion in chapter 6 is that "Christian belief can have warrant . . . produced in the believer by the internal instigation of the Holy Spirit, endorsing the teaching of Scripture."[68] This is more than a narrowly intellectual belief—this kind of faith is both cognitive and affective.

Plantinga cites numerous examples of genuine faith, selected from many biblical passages, with further examples from Martin Luther and Jonathan Edwards; even at the level of a starting point: "By faith we understand that the worlds were prepared by the word of God" (Heb. 11:3 NRSV).

Propositions arrived at by inference are quite different from the whole array of Christian faith and belief, which may be challenged by what Plantinga calls "defeaters." Defeaters constitute an important part of Reformed epistemology, and nearly a third of the book *Knowledge and Christian Belief,* as well as the last part of *Warranted Christian Belief,* concerns this subject.[69] Defeaters are today used more widely in philosophy of religion. They refer to the vulnerability or liability of beliefs to criticism. If the defeater is strong or convincing, such beliefs become reduced, weaker, or even no longer justified as valid. The term seems to be derived from H. L. A. Hart in the context of

---

64. Plantinga, *Knowledge and Christian Belief,* 59 (emphasis added).
65. Ibid., 60.
66. Calvin, *Institutes,* 3.2.18 (emphasis added).
67. Plantinga, *Knowledge and Christian Belief,* 69.
68. Ibid., 72.
69. Ibid., 92–127; and Plantinga, *Warranted Christian Belief,* 357–499.

philosophy of law and legal contracts. It is often asked: are legal rules "defeasible"?[70] The notion of propositional defeat is taken up more broadly and features as a major tool in Plantinga's epistemology.

In *Warranted Christian Belief*, Plantinga further explains the nature of defeaters: "Given belief in the defeating proposition, you can retain the belief in the defeating proposition only at the cost of irrationality. There are also *warrant* defeaters that are not rationality defeaters."[71] He then considers a sequence of possible defeaters for Christian belief. One concerns attacks on the divine inspiration of Scripture, especially in radical biblical criticism since the Enlightenment. Plantinga rightly points here to the varieties of biblical criticism from Ernst Troeltsch and others to more moderate critics today.[72] He addresses the problems of pluralism and postmodernism, including historical conditioning and finitude (*Geschichtlichkeit*, often translated "historicality"). He also addresses the pragmatic arguments of Richard Rorty.[73] Finally, he responds to the key problem of suffering and evil, which is probably the most frequently cited argument against the validity of Christian belief in God as almighty, all knowing, and good.[74]

Although this concerns the kind of area that we normally consider in the philosophy of religion or apologetics, it is important not to confuse this with traditional apologetics or natural theology, in Plantinga. Such arguments can perform very different functions.

Kevin Diller, whose recent book identifies common ground between Plantinga and Barth, writes that Plantinga's conception of natural theology is "much more narrowly defined than the natural theology debated by Barth and Brunner."[75] Plantinga defines natural theology simply as "the attempt to prove or demonstrate the existence of God." But as we have seen, he prefers the witness of testimony to that of inference. In their joint rejection of natural theology (in Plantinga's sense), Plantinga and Barth indeed share common ground. On the other hand, Plantinga's view resonates with Brun-

---

70. H. L. A. Hart, "The Description of Responsibility and Rights," in *Readings in Philosophy and Law*, ed. Herbert Morris (Stanford: Stanford University Press, 1961), 143–48.

71. Plantinga, *Warranted Christian Belief*, 359.

72. Ibid., 390–421.

73. Ibid., 422–57.

74. Ibid., 458–99.

75. Kevin Diller, *Theology's Theological Dilemma: How Karl Barth and Alvin Plantinga Promote a Unified Response* (Downers Grove: IVP Academic, 2014), 196.

ner's distinctive term "eristics," as the defensive rational discussion simply of arguments that oppose the Christian faith.[76] Brunner contrasts apologetics, which serve to defend the Christian faith, with eristics, which merely counters objections to belief. Plantinga's appeal to the gradual building up of a system or network of beliefs, in contrast to inferences from a single proposition, is not a thousand miles away from Wittgenstein's emphasis: both on a nest of propositions and on hinge propositions. This is in spite of admittedly huge differences between them on other matters. Plantinga is concerned with distinctively Christian knowledge and belief. On affinities with Barth, Diller seems to have succeeded, as the preface written by Plantinga suggests.

---

76. Emil Brunner, *Christian Doctrine of God* (London: Lutterworth, 1949), 98.

CHAPTER 8

Eschatological Certainty and the Holy Spirit

Eschatological Verification and Eschatological Revelation

The two parts of the chapter title are closely related. Oscar Cullmann declares: "The Holy Spirit is nothing else than the anticipation of the end in the present."[1] Joseph Fison makes almost exactly the same point.[2] Yet at the same time Cullmann writes: "The time tension is manifested in the church through the continuance of sin, which nevertheless has already been defeated by the Spirit."[3] To Cullmann's comments about sin, we might also add human fallibility, finitude, and uncertainty, which may be as characteristic of the present era, rather than the future, as is the continuance of sin.

Christians, Cullmann argues, still sin and still die in the present era; yet: "Man *is* that which he *will become* only in the future, that is, he is already sinless, already holy, although this becomes a reality only in the future."[4] Once again, Fison repeats almost exactly the same words: "We are to 'become what we are'—that is the secret of the Pauline understanding of the way of salvation."[5] Might we not say the same about certainty? In the present,

---

1. Oscar Cullmann, *Christ and Time: The Primitive Conception of Time and History* (London: SCM, 1951), 72.

2. Joseph E. Fison, *The Blessing of the Holy Spirit* (London: Longmans, Green, 1950), 122–26.

3. Cullmann, *Christ and Time*, 155.

4. Ibid., 75 (emphasis original).

5. Fison, *Blessing of the Holy Spirit*, 133.

humankind is fallible and uncertain; yet in terms of what the Christian will become, certainty is provisionally anticipated "in Christ" (in the life of the believer) and less provisionally in the future.

Alvin Plantinga makes much of the initiative of the Holy Spirit. Wolfhart Pannenberg also makes much of the future and its "provisional" anticipation in the present. Among his many writings, in his essay "Eschatology and the Experience of Meaning," he declares: "What formerly seemed insignificant may perhaps appear later as of fundamental importance. . . . The final significance of events of our life, Dilthey once said, can be measured only at the end of our lives."[6] The end will bring "a manifestation of the totality of meaning."[7] He explains this more succinctly in his early writings: "Only in the light of the end does the revelation of God become fully understandable."[8] He adds: "The eschatological event . . . binds history into a whole."[9] Anything approaching certainty would require the entire context of history as a whole, even if provisionally anticipated in Christ and the Holy Spirit.

A more directly philosophical approach to the same problem of eschatology (alongside Dilthey) comes from a writer in a different tradition, namely John Hick. In at least four works Hick wrote on "eschatological verification."[10] Hick introduces his concept of eschatological verification with a parable. Two people are traveling along the road that one of them believes leads to a celestial city. The other believes that it leads nowhere. Neither has been along this way before. So neither can be certain about his or her destination. Both meet with hardships, dangers, and places of refreshment. The one who believes he is on a journey to a celestial city regards the hardships as obstacles or trials to be overcome and the places of refreshment as encouragement to persevere. The other person sees these as inevitable parts of a random and aimless ramble, which they encounter by sheer luck or

6. Wolfhart Pannenberg, *Basic Questions in Theology* (London: SCM, 1970–73), 3.201.

7. Ibid., 3.205.

8. Wolfhart Pannenberg, "The Revelation of God in Jesus of Nazareth," in *New Frontiers in Theology: Theology as History*, ed. James M. Robinson and J. B. Cobb (New York: Harper & Row, 1967), 101–33 at 113.

9. Ibid., 122.

10. John Hick, *Faith and Knowledge* (London: Macmillan, 1988 [orig. 1957]), 176–99; idem, *Philosophy of Religion*, 4th ed. (Englewood Cliffs, NJ: Prentice Hall, 1990 [orig. 1963]), 103–5; idem, "Theology and Verification," *Theology Today* 17 (1960): 12–31; and idem (ed.), *The Existence of God* (New York: Macmillan, 1964), 253–74.

The Two Roads

fate. During the journey itself, what divides their way of regarding things is not a matter of experience. Neither attitude can be tested by verification or falsification in relation to evidence or experience, for they have neither. But when they come in sight of their destination it becomes apparent then which of them has been right all along, and which of the two has been wrong all the time. Hick concludes: "Their opposed interpretations of the road constituted genuinely rival assertions. . . . [Now] guaranteed retrospectively by a future crux."[11]

Hick's idea of eschatological verification goes back to an essay by John Wisdom (1904–93), in which he also expounded a parable to illustrate his point. Wisdom first published "The Invisible Gardener" in 1944–45 in the wake of logical positivism.[12] The parable describes two people returning to their long-neglected garden. They find among the weeds some surprisingly vigorous plants. One person who returned says to his companion: "It must be that the gardener has been coming and doing something about those weeds." The other disagrees, and the two argue at length. They keep watch, but never see a gardener. The believer suspects it may be an invisible gardener, so they hire bloodhounds to keep watch. Nothing causes the dogs to respond. Against the believer's tenacity, the skeptic asks how an invisible, intangible, soundless, odorless gardener differs from a merely imaginary gardener. It is a thinly veiled description of the believer's dilemma about the existence of God.

There have been numerous responses to the parable. Flew claims that the parable has been reprinted no less than forty times. It set the tone for much twentieth-century philosophy and debate with Christian believers since about 1955. Flew includes "Theology and Falsification" in his collection *New Essays in Philosophical Theology*.[13] Responses included negative ones from Flew, and positive ones for belief from R. M. Hare (1919–2002) and Basil Mitchell (1917–2011), formerly Nolloth Professor of the Philosophy of

---

11. Hick, *Faith and Knowledge*, 178.

12. John Wisdom, "Gods," *Proceedings of the Aristotelian Society* 65 (1944–45): 45–46; reprinted in *Logic and Language*, ed. Antony Flew (Oxford: Blackwell, 1951). The following summary is adapted from Peter Wenz's treatment in *Abortion Rights as Religious Freedom* (Philadelphia: Temple University Press, 1992), 368.

13. Antony Flew and Alasdair MacIntyre (eds.), *New Essays in Philosophical Theology* (London: SCM, 1955), 96–130.

the Christian Religion, at Oxford. Mitchell, for example, suggests that two further strategies of faith would be either to retain the belief as an article of faith or to accept the issue as hypothetical, to be confirmed or disconfirmed in the light of subsequent experience.[14] There are numerous other responses in philosophical journals. Hick takes up, as it were, Mitchell's second alternative as his starting point. The debate also explains why the term "verification" is important to him. For roughly twenty years (1950–70) this issue was a major one in philosophical theology on both sides of the debate, especially in Britain.

On the basis of Christian faith, the believer believes that, at some time in the future, the criterion of the dilemma about belief will become, in effect, "experiential and evidential." Meanwhile Hick speaks of this experience as being relevant "retrospectively."

In a very different context, Pannenberg speaks of the relevance of the end in an anticipatory or provisional way. This emphasis, Pannenberg says, provides an important respect in which his eschatology remains different from that of Hegel.[15] Hick believes that eschatological verification suffices "to render the choice between theism and atheism a real, and not merely empty or verbal, choice.... The universe as envisaged by the theist, then, differs as a totality from the universe envisioned by the atheist."[16] This totality invites relevant comparison with what we have seen in both Wittgenstein and Plantinga about the basis of certainty.

Both Hick and Pannenberg, in very different ways, emphasize the continuity of identity between an earthly human being facing death and the raised (or surviving) human being who experiences eschatological verification or confirmation. Hick tends to use the philosopher's notion of "continued personal existence after death."[17] Pannenberg uses the more biblical and correct theological language of "eschatological resurrection to life."[18] In all the

---

14. Basil Mitchell, "Theology and Falsification," in *New Essays in Philosophical Theology*, ed. Antony Flew and Alasdair MacIntyre (London: SCM, 1955), 103–5.

15. Wolfhart Pannenberg, *Systematic Theology* (Edinburgh: T&T Clark/Grand Rapids: Eerdmans, 1991–98), 3.532–33.

16. Hick, *Faith and Knowledge*, 178.

17. Ibid., 179.

18. Pannenberg, *Systematic Theology*, 2.349–63; idem, *Jesus—God and Man* (London: SCM, 1968), 88 106, 344 49; cf. Anthony C. Thiselton *Life after Death* (Grand Rapids: Eerdmans, 2012), 111–28 = British edition, *The Last Things* (London: SPCK, 2012), 136–44.

sources cited in this chapter, the continuity of the self through death and new life is defended and affirmed, just as Paul defends it through the analogy of the seed and fruit in 1 Corinthians 15:35–44 and in other ways. The self may be transformed into a different mode of existence, but it remains the same self. In philosophy the best defense of continuity of identity that I know is that by Paul Ricoeur (1913–2005). Many unbelievers claim that the self this side of the grave is "the only self of which we know. . . . The empirical self, the walking, talking, acting . . . individual."[19] But in an exceedingly complex and sophisticated discussion, Ricoeur shows how continuity of identity can make sense.

Ricoeur reviews philosophical attempts to make continuity of identity intelligible, from John Locke to the present.[20] He first looks at P. F. Strawson's *Individuals*, which he finds helpful but still unsatisfactory. He then introduces semantic questions about "sameness." Ricoeur examines J. L. Austin, Paul Grice, and the personal conditions of speech acts and communication, with further reference to Wittgenstein.[21] He next turns to consider the personal "who" of semantics and of personal action, with reference to G. E. M. Anscombe and Donald Davidson.[22] He then considers personal agency and explores "personal identity and narrative identity." This provides a hopeful approach to the identity of the self, partly because narratives involve talking about *persons*, not just things. Ricoeur writes: "Personal identity . . . can be articulated only in the temporal dimension of human existence" and in narrative in order "to confront head-on the distinction between sameness and selfhood."[23] At this point he draws on his own three-volume *Time and Narrative* to explain his notion of "emplotments" and to underline the personal interconnection of events depicted in a narrative.[24] Emplotment reveals the dialectic between necessity and probability, and various strategies of communication. He discusses the narrative action and characterization of Vladimir Propp and A. J. Greimas.

After this significant prolegomenon, Ricoeur expounds his more distinctive view of what "requires a person [to be] *accountable for his or her*

---

19. Hick, *Faith and Knowledge*, 179.
20. Paul Ricoeur, *Oneself as Another* (Chicago: University of Chicago Press, 1992), 27–202.
21. Ibid., 40–55.
22. Ibid., 56–87.
23. Ibid., 113–68 at 114.
24. Ibid., 140.

acts."[25] He adds: "Narrative function is not without *ethical* implications."[26] This overcomes David Hume's belief that the self is no more than a bundle of perceptions. I often illustrate the effects of accountability to students in terms of the analogy of paying into a fund for superannuation or a pension. The one who will collect the pension after retirement is "the same person" as the one who paid in during his earlier life. The thirty-year-old may even have disliked the lifestyle and appearance of the seventy-or-eighty-year-old who draws the pension! But they are the same person, who is entitled to draw on the penalties and privileges won in earlier years. In theology all this reaches a climax in the concept of the last judgment. Paul the apostle wrote: "We walk by faith, not by sight. . . . All of us must appear before the judgment seat of Christ, so that each may receive recompense for what has been done in the body, whether good or evil" (2 Cor. 5:7, 10 NRSV).

Ricoeur spends the remainder of his book, and indeed the rest of his life, addressing ethical questions and especially the question of justice. These bring together his interest in narrative, his concerns about time, and his concerns about personal identity. In the remainder of *Oneself as Another*, he considers Aristotle on virtue and, like Pannenberg, "totality or complete-ness."[27] Only when we view the whole, completed picture can we fully understand the truth of what we are able then to see. Ricoeur's exploration of ethics includes considering solicitude in Martin Heidegger and hospitality and other virtues in Emmanuel Lévinas, especially in the latter's *Otherwise than Being* and *Totality and Infinity*.[28] Between *Oneself as Another* and his death in 2005, Ricoeur's works include *The Just*, *Reflections on the Just*, and *Living Up to Death*.[29] This concern was lifelong: Ricoeur was concerned with finitude, fallibility, and guilt, in his earliest works: *Freedom and Nature* (1950) and *Fallible Man* (1960).

To return to our immediate subject, Hick also emphasizes the continuity of the self in resurrection, alluding to "the spiritual body" (Greek *sōma pneu-*

---

25. Ibid., 151 (emphasis added).

26. Ibid., 163–202 at 163.

27. Ibid., 187, 211.

28. Ibid., 322–29, 357–40.

29. Paul Ricoeur, *The Just* (Chicago: University of Chicago Press, 2000); idem, *Reflections on the Just* (Chicago: University of Chicago Press, 2007); and idem, *Living Up to Death* (Chicago: University of Chicago Press, 2009).

matikon; 1 Cor. 15:44). But Hick does not warm to the notion that before we reach the end of the journey, the existence of God and the Christian system of belief is no more than "a tentatively adopted hypothesis which awaits deification after death."[30] Hick is correct to claim that Christian faith is more than "a tentatively adopted hypothesis," and he criticizes I. M. Crombie on this basis.[31] I earlier noted Oscar Cullmann's assertion that "man *is* that which he *will become* only in the future" (emphasis original), with which Joseph Fison concurs. Pannenberg and most New Testament scholars hold this more positive view of faith based on our final destiny in the new creation.

Hick calls this "faith which is so complete that it leaves no room for doubt," although he also rightly adds: "Faith is in practice a variable state" that might undergo periods of doubt in given situations.[32] Both Hick and Pannenberg regard the revelation of God in Jesus of Nazareth as playing a decisive part in shaping Christian faith. Pannenberg well sums up the tension of the present and the future in the following words: "Jesus of Nazareth is the final revelation of God, because the end of history appeared in him. It did so both in his eschatological message and in his resurrection from the dead. However, he can be understood to be God's final revelation only in connection with the whole of history as mediated by the history of Israel. . . . *All history receives its due light from him.*"[33]

Pannenberg hastens to say that the emphasis on history bypasses Bultmann and the Neo-Kantian dualism between word and event. History reveals, he says, "an intertwining both of prophetic words and of events."[34] Pannenberg writes: "The expected general resuscitation of the dead at the end had clearly occurred in Jesus' case. . . . This presupposes a preliminary knowledge. . . . The eschatological event . . . binds history into a whole. . . . Against this [i.e., Bultmann's view] we must reinstate today the original unity of the facts and their meaning. . . . Knowledge is not a stage beyond faith, but leads into faith."[35]

---

30. Hick, *Faith and Knowledge*, 180–91.

31. Ibid., 194; and I. M. Crombie, "Theology and Falsification," in *New Essays in Philosophical Theology*, ed. Antony Flew and Alasdair MacIntyre (London: SCM, 1955), 109–30.

32. Hick, *Faith and Knowledge*, 195.

33. Pannenberg, "Revelation of God," 125.

34. Ibid., 120.

35. Ibid., 113–14, 119, 120, 127, 129.

The Definitive Last Judgment in Theology

One feature that stands out in biblical passages about the judgment of God, especially in contrast with today, is the joy and exultation with which the people of God awaited and expected that judgment. This is especially evident in the Old Testament. The psalmist wrote: "Let the heavens be glad, and let the earth rejoice. . . . Then shall all the trees of the forest sing for joy before the LORD; for he is coming, for he is coming to judge the earth" (Ps. 96:11–13 NRSV). Another psalm repeats this emphasis of joyful anticipation concerning the judgment: "Let the nations be glad and sing for joy, for you [God] judge the peoples with equity" (67:4 NRSV).

Why do the Old Testament people of God long for God's judgment? There is no suggestion here of a head teacher or principal announcing examination results. God's people and even the nations long for the end of oppression, ignorance, frustration, doubt, deception, seduction, illusion, and the reign of tyrants. At the final judgment God will vindicate the oppressed publicly and definitively. Psalm 98 makes this clear: God "has revealed his vindication in the sight of nations. . . . Make a joyful noise to the LORD, all the earth; break forth into joyous song . . . for he is coming to judge the earth. He will judge the world with righteousness, and the peoples with equity (98:2, 4, 9 NRSV). As king of all creation, God will put to right all wrongs, including vindicating believers for whom faith, not sight, sustained their belief hitherto, sometimes while others mocked them (2 Cor. 5:7; Heb. 11:1–2, 13).

God's judgment includes political and intellectual spheres as well as others. Liberation theologians, including José Porfirio Miranda, frequently expound God's "judgment" (Hebrew mišpāṭ) in terms of justice at this point. In the world of New Testament scholarship, Peter Stuhlmacher, Karl Kartelge, and Ernst Käsemann take up this point. Käsemann, among the others, relates the judgment to "God's sovereignty over the world, revealing itself eschatologically in Jesus."[36] Artur Weiser comments on Psalm 98:9: "The yearning for God and the absolute certainty of God's gracious will prove themselves to be too strong to be overshadowed by fear."[37] On this aspect

36. Ernst Käsemann, "The Righteousness of God in Paul," in *New Testament Questions of Today* (London: SCM, 1969), 168–82 at 180.
37. Artur Weiser, *The Psalms: A Commentary* (London: SCM, 1962), 639.

Stephen Travis writes: "The emphasis on restorative justice is not on 'paying back' the offender, but on positively 'putting right' what has gone wrong between the offender and the victim."[38] In Isaiah, God is "a righteous God and a Savior" (Isa. 45:21 NRSV).

Nevertheless, does the last judgment provide knowledge, certainty, and the removal of doubt? Many of the parables of Jesus speak of the ambiguity of the present, which is to be resolved in the future. In plain speech, Jesus asserts: "Nothing is covered up that will not be uncovered, and nothing secret that will not become known" (Matt. 10:26 NRSV). Joachim Jeremias comments: "Conditions are reversed; *what is hidden becomes manifest*."[39] Then in Matthew 13:47-49 different kinds of fish are caught from the sea, but "at the end . . . angels will come out and separate the evil from the righteous" (NRSV), or in parabolic terms the good fish will be separated from the bad. The parable of the good seed sown among the weeds offers another example: "Let both grow together until the harvest; and at harvest time I will . . . gather the wheat into my barns" (13:24-30 NRSV).

Paul is no less clear than Jesus. He writes: "Do not pronounce judgment before the time, before the Lord comes, who will bring to light the things now hidden in darkness and will disclose the purposes of the heart" (1 Cor. 4:5 NRSV). Paul utterly acknowledges his ignorance about the success or otherwise of his ministry; we simply cannot tell "before the time." He comments: "I do not even judge myself. I am not aware of anything against myself, but I am not thereby acquitted. It is the Lord who judges me" (4:3-4 NRSV). The Corinthians, or at least many of them, insisted on jumping the gun and thought that they "reigned as kings" and regarded the apostles literally as "scum" (4:8-13). They tried to evaluate life and truth in midprocess, as if this could be done today by judging a building or a work of art simply in the middle of construction.

There are a number of parallels to this in Paul. Famously, in 1 Corinthians 13:12, Paul declares: "Now we see in a mirror, dimly, but then we will see face to face. Now I know only in part; then I will know fully, even as I have been fully known" (NRSV). "Through a mirror" (Greek *di' esop-*

---

38. Stephen H. Travis, *Christ and the Judgement of God* (Milton Keynes: Paternoster, 2008), 8.

39. Joachim Jeremias, *The Parables of Jesus* (London: SCM, 1963), 221 (emphasis added).

trou) describes the means of perception; "dimly" (Greek *en ainigmati*) signifies obscurity, puzzle, or even distortion. Corinth was well known for the manufacture of bronze mirrors. Slightly concave or convex mirrors would readily promote a distorted image. Even good, well-polished, mirrors could still be indistinct and certainly offered indirect vision. In the Platonic tradition, mirrors symbolized vision.[40] Knowledge was "part by part" (Greek *ek merous*), that is, limited to fragments of particular points of view, which should not be pressed. "Face to face" reflects the Hebrew *pānîm 'el-pānîm*, which indicates intimacy with God. Knowledge is just as complete as God's knowledge of me. Elsewhere I write: "Perfect 'knowledge' is not merely by inference or deduction."[41]

Similarly in 1 Corinthians 4:5, on the future day, as in Romans 2:16, "God judges human secrets"; hence in the present, "Let us no more pass judgment on one another," as in Colossians 2:16-19. We simply do not have knowledge, let alone certainty, to engage in criticizing others in the present. We do not know the whole story. On that day, the Lord will shed light upon (Greek future indicative of *phōtizō*) the hidden things (*ta krypta*) hitherto concealed and protected by darkness. This will include the hidden motivations or wishes (*tas boulas*) of hearts, some of which are hidden even from ourselves. As Bultmann, and especially Theissen, correctly argue, "heart" denotes or includes what today, after Freud, we call the "unconscious."[42]

A third key witness in the New Testament is the anonymous author of the Epistle to the Hebrews, who was no mean theologian. Eschatology, says C. K. Barrett, is the "determining event" in Hebrews.[43] The addressees are on a pilgrimage to the new Jerusalem. On this earth in the present, Christians have "no abiding city; they seek a city which is to come" (Heb. 13:14). Ernst Käsemann and Robert Jewett focus especially on this perspective.[44]

---

40. Anthony C. Thiselton, *First Corinthians: A Commentary on the Greek Text*, New International Greek Testament Commentary (Grand Rapids: Eerdmans, 2000), 1068-70.

41. Anthony C. Thiselton, *1 Corinthians: A Shorter Exegetical and Pastoral Commentary* (Grand Rapids: Eerdmans, 2006), 232.

42. Rudolf Bultmann, *Theology of the New Testament* (London: SCM, 1952), 1.223-27; Gerd Theissen, *Psychological Aspects of Theology* (Edinburgh: T&T Clark, 1987), 57-114, 228-319.

43. C. K. Barrett, "The Eschatology of the Epistle to the Hebrews," in *The Background of the New Testament and Its Eschatology: In Honour of C. H. Dodd*, ed. W. D. Davies and D. Daube (Cambridge: Cambridge University Press, 1956), 363-93 at 366.

44. Ernst Käsemann, *The Wandering People of God: An Investigation of the Letter to the*

The people are the "city" or destination; they belong to the future and to the realm of genuineness (Greek *alēthina*) in contrast to "shadows" or "copies" (Greek *hypodeigmata*). God reveals himself to the Old Testament believers in ways that F. F. Bruce calls "partial and piecemeal" (Greek *polymerōs kai polytropōs*; Heb. 1:1).[45] Jesus, the new "Joshua," leads the people to the promised goal (4:8-9). God's revelation of himself rests, once again, on promise (6:13, 17; 7:21): "Faith is the assurance [*hypostasis*] of things hoped for, the conviction [*elenchos*] of things not seen" (11:1 NRSV). Old Testament believers base their faith on the promise of God for the future, from Abel to Abraham, from Moses to the judges, and in the intertestamental writings (11:4-39). Hence, the writer urges: "Let us run with perseverance the race that is set before us" (12:1 NRSV). The pilgrims' journey is "to Mount Zion and to the city of the living God, the heavenly Jerusalem" (12:22 NRSV). The future will offer certainty, for it is "a kingdom that cannot be shaken" (12:28 NRSV).

First Peter and John share this future perspective, even if in the Gospel of John the fulfillment of eschatology in the present is also emphasized. E. G. Selwyn comments on 1 Peter: Christians "live in grace but not yet in glory."[46] Although he often emphasizes the experience of eternal life in the present, the writer of John does not minimize the future aspect. Raymond Brown comments: "The establishment . . . of the kingdom is yet to come, and the church is orientated toward the future *basileia*. . . . There is a future vision of glory."[47] Jesus declares: "I should lose nothing . . . but raise it [my body, the people of God] up on the last day" (John 6:39-40 NRSV).

In historical and systematic theology the "double polarity" of the present and the future in the New Testament is clear. Paul Tillich, for one, emphasizes the ambiguities of life in the present. Human fallenness suggests disintegration, fragmentation, lack of stability, partial knowledge, and estrange-

---

Hebrews (Minneapolis: Augsburg, 1984), esp. 26-37; Robert Jewett, *Letter to Pilgrims: A Commentary on the Epistle to the Hebrews* (Cleveland: Pilgrim, 1981).

45. F. F. Bruce, *The Epistle to the Hebrews* (London: Marshall, Morgan, and Scott, 1964), 1-2.

46. E. G. Selwyn, "Eschatology in 1 Peter," in *The Background of the New Testament and Its Eschatology: In Honour of C. H. Dodd*, ed. W. D. Davies and D. Daube (Cambridge: Cambridge University Press, 1956), 394-41 at 396.

47. Raymond Brown, *The Gospel according to John*, Anchor Bible 29 (New York: Doubleday, 1971), cxvii-cxviii.

ment from God. But this will be overcome in the future.[48] God's judgment, he says, will defeat evolution in "the eternal conquest of the negative."[49] In the earliest years of the church, Irenaeus (ca. 130–ca. 200) famously held to the notion of Christ's "recapitulation" of all things in Christ, largely on the basis of Ephesians 1:10. The Greek term *anakephalaiōsis* means "to sum up, recapitulate, or complete" and is usually understood as referring to a future goal.[50] In our own day this theme is taken up by Jürgen Moltmann (born 1926), who speaks of the restoration of all things as their transformation and transfiguration at the end.[51] Indeed his entire book *The Coming of God* expounds Christian eschatology. What will pass away, he declares, is "the 'form of this world'"; the world as God's creation will be transformed in accordance with God's declaration and promise: "I am making all things new. . . . It is done! I am the Alpha and the Omega, the beginning and the end" (Rev. 21:5–6 NRSV).[52]

Wolfhart Pannenberg wholeheartedly places eschatology in a prominent and central place in his systematic theology: "Grounding eschatology in the concept of promise is correct, inasmuch as eschatological hope can rest only on God himself."[53] Pannenberg, in this respect, unreservedly endorses the words of Catholic theologian Karl Rahner (1904–84). According to both of them (in virtually identical words): "If the future means the future of salvation as the fulfillment of the *whole* person, then knowledge of this future, regardless of its hiddenness, is constitutive for human life as it now is. For *we can understand our present . . . [which is] a fragmentary reality, only in the light of our knowledge of its ultimate wholeness.*"[54] Pannenberg adds: "Extrapolation from knowledge of possible wholeness . . . is part of our historical understanding. . . . The promises put the human present, with all the pain of its incompleteness and failure, in the light of the future of God that comes to us as our salvation."[55]

---

48. Paul Tillich, *Systematic Theology* (London: Nisbet, 1964), 3.34–113, 153–59, 424–31.

49. Ibid., 431.

50. Irenaeus, *Against Heresies* 5.20.2; 5.21.1–2.

51. Jürgen Moltmann, *The Coming of God: Christian Eschatology* (London: SCM, 1996), 294.

52. Ibid., 271.

53. Pannenberg, *Systematic Theology*, 3.539.

54. Ibid., 3.543; and Karl Rahner, *Theological Investigations* (London: Darton, Longman & Todd, 1973), 4.331, 311 (emphasis added).

55. Pannenberg, *Systematic Theology*, 3.544–45.

Eschatology and the last judgment have always featured in Christian theology, except within a particular stream of thought, often known as liberalism, between the Enlightenment and the nineteenth century.[56] Pannenberg, among others, completely vindicates the notion that absolute certainty is bound up with the full revelation of the whole of history and the end. Meanwhile, "we see in the mirror, dimly" (1 Cor. 13:12 NRSV), when any approximation to knowledge, let alone certainty, remains fragmentary, finite, and to some extent distorted by finitude and sin. What we know now depends on what can be anticipated in Christ, from the standpoint of the end. Then the last judgment of God will be definitive, authoritative, and incapable of revision. As Pannenberg declares, definitive knowledge and evaluation depend on an understanding of the whole, which embraces all possible contexts and all of human history. Kierkegaard often stresses, by contrast, that a mere finite individual can have little more than a fragmentary point of view. If he is right, a measure of pluralism, distortion, and relative ignorance in the present should not take us by surprise.

The Holy Spirit and the Anticipation of the End

I noted at the beginning of this chapter Cullmann's memorable comment: "The Holy Spirit is the anticipation of the end in the present." The Holy Spirit transforms us into what God has in store for us as our future destiny, and that transformation gradually begins now. This is why Paul calls the Holy Spirit "the firstfruits" (Greek *aparchē*; Rom. 8:23) of our future inheritance. Elsewhere he speaks of the Spirit as the "first installment" of our inheritance (2 Cor. 1:22; Greek *arrabōn*). Danker translates *arrabōn* as "payment of part of a purchase price in advance, first installment, deposit, down payment, pledge."[57] Like a deposit, it guarantees more of the same yet to come, of which the present possession remains only a fraction. In 2 Corinthians 5:5 the Spirit is depicted as a guarantee (*arrabōn*). In New Testament scholarship

---

56. This point was made emphatically by James P. Martin, *The Last Judgement in Protestant Theology from Orthodoxy to Ritschl* (Edinburgh: Oliver & Boyd, 1963). An outline of patristic eschatology is provided by Brian E. Daley, *The Hope of the Early Church: A Handbook of Patristic Eschatology* (Cambridge: Cambridge University Press, 1991).

57. BDAG 134.

the importance of this aspect of Paul is not disputed and finds expression, for example, in H. Gunkel, N. Q. Hamilton, Gordon D. Fee, F. Horn, and F. Philip, among many others.[58] Hamilton comments: "The centre of gravity lies in the future. . . . 'He who sows to the Spirit will of the Holy Spirit reap eternal life'" (Gal. 6:8).[59]

This aspect has special importance in view of two closely related themes. First, we have seen in Plantinga and others that it is the Holy Spirit who will bring a Christian certainty to the believer. Paul reminds us: "Then shall I know even as I am known" (1 Cor. 13:12), that is, as God knows me. But, as Torrance and others stress, the Holy Spirit is the epistemological agent of God's self-revelation. We have also seen, especially from Pannenberg, the second theme that in the present this remains provisional and anticipatory, pending future fulfillment. Certainty, during the present, remains, for the Christian, certainty of faith—not of sight. In the future, especially in the light of the last judgment and an even fuller gift of the Holy Spirit, it will be transformed into actual certainty, in public sight. Along the lines expounded by Hick, retrospectively we shall be assured of the vindication of our journey and our God-given faith.

Hamilton also observes that in Paul there is a threefold connection between the Holy Spirit and the end. First, the Holy Spirit is the agent through whom God raised Christ and will raise Christian believers (Rom. 8:11). Second, the Spirit implements, or brings home to the believer, the reality of God's promises for the future (4:13–21 and elsewhere). Third, the inheritance of redemption, which Paul mentions at least five times, is also fulfilled through the agency of the Holy Spirit (Greek *klēronomeō*; 1 Cor. 6:9–10; 15:50; Gal. 5:21; Eph. 5:5; and elsewhere). James Hester and N. T. Wright, among others, expound the theme of inheritance and the Spirit's part in this.[60]

The Holy Spirit gives new, ever-fresh life and will sustain this ongoing life of the raised believer. This is part of the resurrection mode of existence.

---

58. H. Gunkel, *The Influence of the Holy Spirit* (Minneapolis: Fortress, 2008), 82; N. Q. Hamilton, *The Holy Spirit and Eschatology in Paul*, Scottish Journal of Theology Occasional Paper 6 (Edinburgh: Oliver & Boyd, 1957), 19–21; Gordon D. Fee, *God's Empowering Presence: The Holy Spirit in the Letters of Paul* (Milton Keynes: Paternoster/Peabody: Hendrickson, 1994–95), 287–96, 572–75.

59. Hamilton, *Holy Spirit and Eschatology in Paul*, 19.

60. James D. Hester, *Paul's Concept of Inheritance* (Edinburgh: Oliver & Boyd, 1958); N. T. Wright, "The New Inheritance according to Paul," *Bible Review* 14.3 (1998): n.p.

Long ago in 1909, Henry B. Swete asserted: "The resurrection of the body is so far from being the last work of the indwelling Spirit that it [i.e., he] will be the starting point of a new creativity of spiritual life."[61] Thus the Holy Spirit will animate an enhanced, ongoing, ever-dynamic, untarnished existence in the postresurrection world. As Roy Harrisville argues, the new will reflect both continuity and contrast with the old manner of existence, or preresurrection body.[62]

The resurrection body (Greek *sōma pneumatikon*; 1 Cor. 15:44) is more than physical, but certainly not immaterial. It includes whatever is counterpart to the physical in the superearthly realm. At all events, in 1 Cor. 15:44 "spiritual" means wholly in accordance with the Holy Spirit: with his power, holiness, and nature.[63] It is utterly dependent on the power of God. The word "spiritual" does not indicate material out of which the mode of existence is composed, but denotes a mode of existence characterized by the energy, purity, and ever-fresh renewal of the Holy Spirit. It is certainly not static perfection, as envisaged by Aquinas under the influence of Aristotle. "Perfect" can characterize different stages of existence. A perfect baby has different qualities from a perfect adult. The splendor of the new life contrasts with the weakness, decay, and weakening capacities of aging, illness, and sin that stand in contrast with it in 15:42–43.[64]

To quote Hamilton again: "Apart from the doctrine of the Spirit, this break-in of the future into the present agrees with Paul's use of other eschatological terms. Paul describes the present time as "this age" (Greek *ho aiōn houtos*; Rom. 12:2; 1 Cor. 1:20; 2:6; 3:18; 2 Cor. 4:4; Gal. 1:4)."[65] The future age is mentioned as "the age to come." The term *aparchē* ("firstfruits") could also denote the first crop of the harvest, which would be consecrated to God. Paul uses this as a major concept in his theology of the history of Israel and the church in Romans 16 (cf. Num. 15:18–21). In the larger picture that Paul paints in Romans 8:18–30, he tells us that "creation waits with eager longing

---

61. Henry B. Swete, *The Holy Spirit in the New Testament* (London: Macmillan, 1909), 355.

62. R. A. Harrisville, "The Concept of Newness in the New Testament," *Journal of Biblical Literature* 74 (1955): 69–79.

63. See Thiselton, *First Corinthians*, 1276–81, for a survey of all the main interpretations of the nineteenth and twentieth centuries.

64. N. T. Wright, *The Resurrection of the Son of God* (London: SPCK, 2006), 348–55, rightly adopts this approach.

65. Hamilton, *Holy Spirit and Eschatology in Paul*, 24.

[*apokaradokia*] for the revealing of the children of God" (NRSV). The Greek compound word is intriguing: it consists of *kara* ("head") and *dokeō* ("to seem, imagine") with the intensive preposition *apo*, with a hint of "looking away." Some suggest the English idiom "cranes its neck in anticipation," or as J. B. Phillips translates it: "Creation stands on tiptoe."

In other words, the whole of creation longs to see the glory of God's finished redemption. Romans 8:20–21 concedes that currently creation suffers in bondage to decay.[66] Nevertheless, in C. E. B. Cranfield's words: "The whole magnificent theatre of the universe, together with all the chorus of sub-human life," longs to see the full restoration of humankind.[67] The Spirit assists in the believer's "waiting" (Gal. 3:2; 5:5, 16). Christians press toward the eschatological goal (Phil. 3:11–14) in the strength of the Holy Spirit. They "wait for adoption" (Rom. 8:23 NRSV) and "wait . . . with patience" (8:25 NRSV).

It is not surprising that this period of waiting, and sometimes even suffering, should be a period when "certainty" is merely experienced in faith, not by sight. Believers wait for the definitive vindication of this provisional certainty (in the present), waiting for the final, definitive verdict of the last judgment, when we shall see God "face to face" (1 Cor. 13:12). Then, says Paul, "I will know fully, even as I have been fully known" (13:12 NRSV). The partial, finite, and fragmentary will give way to understanding the whole context and entire picture of God's completed purposes. This will be the enlarged fullest context promised in the Bible and in theology.

Jen. 3

66. On whether or in what sense this implies a cosmic fall, one of the best treatments in terms of both science and theology occurs in John J. Bimson, "Considering a 'Cosmic Fall,'" *Science and Belief* 18 (2006): 63–81.

67. C. E. B. Cranfield, *The Epistle to the Romans*, International Critical Commentary (Edinburgh: T&T Clark, 1975), 1.414.

Bibliography

Alston, William P. *Philosophy of Language*. Englewood Cliffs, NJ: Prentice-Hall, 1964.

Ayer, A. J. "Wittgenstein on Certainty." Pp. 226–45 in *Royal Institute of Philosophy Lectures: 1972/73*. Edited by Godfrey Vesey. London: Macmillan, 1974.

Boyd, Gregory A. *Benefit of Doubt: Breaking the Idol of Certainty*. Grand Rapids: Baker, 2013.

Cioffi-Revella, Claudio. *Politics and Uncertainty: Theory, Models, and Applications*. Cambridge: Cambridge University Press, 1998.

Crombie, I. M. "Theology and Falsification." Pp. 109–30 in *New Essays in Philosophical Theology*. Edited by Antony Flew and Alastair MacIntyre. London: SCM, 1855.

Davidson, Robert. *The Courage to Doubt*. London: SCM/Philadelphia: Trinity, 1983.

Descartes, René. *A Discourse on Method*. London: Dent/New York: Dutton, 1912. Reprinted London: Penguin, 1968 (orig. 1637).

Descartes, René. *The Meditations*. Chicago: Open Court, 1901.

Downing, F. Gerald. "Ambiguity, Ancient Semantics, and Faith." *New Testament Studies* 56 (2010): 139–62.

Erasmus, Desiderius. *The Praise of Folly*. Chicago: Packard, 1946.

Flynn, K. C. "John Henry Newman: The Illative Sense, and the Threat of Scepticism." Draft article online.

Frame, John M., with Vernon Poythress. "Certainty." Pp. 141–45 in *New Dic-

tionary of Christian Apologetics. Edited by W. Campbell-Jack and Gavin McGrath. Leicester: IVP Academic, 2006.

Gigerenzer, Gerd. *Reckoning with Risk: Learning to Live with Uncertainty*. London: Penguin, 2002.

Glock, Hans-Johann. "Certainty." Pp. 76–81 in Glock's *A Wittgenstein Dictionary*. Oxford: Blackwell, 1996.

Hick, John. *Faith and Knowledge*. 2nd ed. London: Macmillan, 1988 (orig. 1957).

Hick, John. *Philosophy of Religion*. 4th ed. Englewood Cliffs, NJ: Prentice Hall, 1990 (orig. 1963).

Hick, John. "Theology and Verification." *Theology Today* 17 (1960): 12–31.

Johnson, Dru. *Biblical Knowing: A Scriptural Epistemology of Error*. Eugene, OR: Cascade, 2013.

Kant, Immanuel. *Critique of Pure Reason*. 2nd revised ed. New York: Macmillan, 1922 (orig. 1896).

Kierkegaard, Søren. *Attack upon "Christendom," 1854–1855*. London: Oxford University Press, 1946.

Kierkegaard, Søren. *Concluding Unscientific Postscript*. Princeton: Princeton University Press, 1941.

Kierkegaard, Søren. *Fear and Trembling* and *The Sickness unto Death*. Princeton: Princeton University Press, 1941.

Kierkegaard, Søren. *The Journals of Søren Kierkegaard*. Oxford: Oxford University Press, 1938.

Kierkegaard, Søren. *The Last Years: Journals, 1853–55*. London: Collins, 1965.

Kierkegaard, Søren. *Philosophical Fragments*. Princeton: Princeton University Press, 1985.

Kierkegaard, Søren. *The Point of View for My Work as an Author*. Oxford: Oxford University Press, 1939. Reprinted New York: Harper, 1962.

Kierkegaard, Søren. *Purity of Heart Is to Will One Thing*. London: Fontana, 1961.

Klein, Peter D. "Certainty." Volume 2/pp. 264–67 in *Routledge Encyclopaedia of Philosophy*. Edited by Edward Craig. London: Routledge, 1998.

Klein, Peter D. *Certainty: A Refutation of Scepticism*. Minneapolis: University of Minnesota Press, 1981.

Kuhn, T. S. "The Logic of Discovery." Pp. 1–23 in *Criticism and the Growth of Knowledge*. Edited by Imre Lakatos and Alan Musgrave. Cambridge: Cambridge University Press, 1970.

Kuhn, T. S. *The Structure of Scientific Revolutions*. 2nd ed. Chicago: Chicago University Press, 1970.

Lakatos, Imre. "Methodology of Scientific Research Programs." Pp. 91–196 in *Criticism and the Growth of Knowledge*. Edited by Imre Lakatos and Alan Musgrave. Cambridge: Cambridge University Press, 1970.

Lakatos, Imre, and Alan Musgrave, eds. *Criticism and the Growth of Knowledge*. Cambridge: Cambridge University Press, 1970.

Locke, John. *An Essay concerning Human Understanding*. Oxford: Clarendon, 1979 (orig. 1689).

Lonergan, Bernard. *Insight: A Study in Human Understanding*. New York: Harper & Row, 1957, 1978.

Lonergan, Bernard. *Method in Theology*. London: Darton, Longman & Todd, 1972.

MacColl, Norman. *The Greek Sceptics from Pyrrho to Sextus*. London: Forgotten Books, 2012 (orig. 1869).

Maxeiner, James R. "Some Realism about Legal Certainty in the Globalisation of the Rule of Law." *Houston Journal of International Law* 27 (2008): 27–46.

Mitchell, Basil. "Theology and Falsification." Pp. 103–5 in *New Essays in Philosophical Theology*. Edited by Antony Flew and Alasdair MacIntyre. London: SCM, 1955.

Moore, G. E. "A Defence of Common Sense." Pp. 32–35 in *Philosophical Papers*. London: Allen & Unwin, 1959.

Moore, G. E. "Proof of My External World." Pp. 147–70 in Moore's *Selected Writings*. London: Routledge, 1993.

Newman, John H. *The Grammar of Assent*. New York: Doubleday, 1955/London: Longmans, 1947 (orig. 1870).

Nichols, Aidan. "John Henry Newman and the Illative Sense: A Reconsideration." *Scottish Journal of Theology* 38 (1985): 347–68.

Oord, Thomas Jay (ed.). *The Polkinghorne Reader: Science, Faith, and the Search for Meaning*. London: SPCK/Templeton, 2010.

Pannenberg, Wolfhart. *Basic Questions in Theology*. 3 volumes. London: SCM, 1970–73.

Pannenberg, Wolfhart. *Jesus—God and Man*. London: SCM, 1968.

Pannenberg, Wolfhart. "The Revelation of God in Jesus of Nazareth." Pp. 101–33 in *New Frontiers in Theology: Theology as History*. Edited by James M. Robinson and J. B. Cobb. New York: Harper & Row, 1967.

Pannenberg, Wolfhart. *Systematic Theology.* 3 volumes. Edinburgh: T&T Clark/Grand Rapids: Eerdmans, 1991–98.

Pannenberg, Wolfhart. *Theology and the Philosophy of Science.* Philadelphia: Westminster, 1976.

Pascal, Blaise. *Pensées.* London: Penguin, 1995 (orig. 1966).

Patrick, Mary Mills. *Sextus Empiricus and Greek Scepticism.* Cambridge: Cambridge University Press, 1899.

Patrick, Mary Mills. *Sextus Empiricus: Outlines of Scepticism.* Edited by J. Annas and J. Barnes. Cambridge: Cambridge University Press, 1994.

Plantinga, Alvin. *Knowledge and Christian Belief.* Grand Rapids: Eerdmans, 2014.

Plantinga, Alvin. "Reformed Epistemology." Pp. 383–89 in *A Companion to Philosophy of Religion.* Edited by Philip L. Quinn and Charles Taliaferro. Oxford: Blackwell, 1999.

Plantinga, Alvin. *Warrant: The Current Debate.* New York: Oxford University Press, 1993.

Plantinga, Alvin. *Warrant and Proper Function.* New York: Oxford University Press, 1994.

Plantinga, Alvin. *Warranted Christian Belief.* New York: Oxford University Press, 2000.

Plantinga, Alvin, and Nicholas Wolterstorff. *Faith and Rationality: Reason and Belief in God.* Notre Dame: University of Notre Dame Press, 1984.

Polanyi, Michael. *Personal Knowledge: Towards a Post-Critical Philosophy.* London: Routledge & Kegan Paul, 1958.

Polkinghorne, John. *Quantum Theory.* Oxford: Oxford University Press, 2002.

Polkinghorne, John. *Science and Religion in Quest of Truth.* London: SPCK, 2011.

Polkinghorne, John. *The Way the World Is.* London: SPCK/Triangle, 1983.

Polkinghorne, John, and Nicholas Beale. *Questions of Truth.* Louisville: Westminster John Knox, 2009.

Popkin, Richard H. *The History of Scepticism from Erasmus to Spinoza.* Berkeley: University of California Press, 1979.

Price, H. H. *Belief.* London: Allen & Unwin/New York: Humanities Press, 1969.

Pritchard, Duncan. "Wittgenstein on Scepticism." Pp. 523–49 in *Oxford*

Handbook to Wittgenstein. Edited by M. McGinn. Oxford: Oxford University Press, 2011.

Quine, Willard van Orman. "Two Dogmas of Empiricism." Pp. 20–46 in Quine's *From a Logical Point of View.* Cambridge: Harvard University Press, 1953. Originally published in *Philosopher's Review* 60 (1951): 20–43.

Ramsey, Ian T. *On Being Sure in Religion.* London: Athlone, 1963.

Ramsey, Ian T. *Religious Language: An Empirical Placing of Theological Phrases.* London: SCM, 1957.

Reed, Barron. "Certainty." In *Stanford Encyclopaedia of Philosophy.* Edited by Edward N. Zalta. 2011. Online at http://plato.stanford.edu/archives/win2011/entries/certainty.

Suk, John. *Not Sure: A Pastor's Journey from Faith to Doubt.* Grand Rapids: Eerdmans, 2011.

Torrance, Thomas F. *God and Rationality.* London: Oxford University Press, 1971.

Torrance, Thomas F. *Theological Science.* London: Oxford University Press, 1969.

Waismann, F. "Verifiability." Pp. 119–23 in *Logic and Language.* Edited by Anthony Flew. Oxford: Blackwell, 1952.

Wittgenstein, Ludwig. *The Blue and Brown Books: Preliminary Studies for the "Philosophical Investigations."* 2nd ed. Oxford: Blackwell, 1969.

Wittgenstein, Ludwig. *On Certainty.* Oxford: Blackwell, 1969.

Wittgenstein, Ludwig. *Philosophical Investigations.* 2nd ed. Oxford: Blackwell, 1967 (orig. 1958).

Wittgenstein, Ludwig. *Zettel.* Oxford: Blackwell, 1967.

Wolterstorff, Nicholas. *John Locke and the Ethics of Belief.* Cambridge: Cambridge University Press, 1996.

Wood, W. Jay. *Epistemology: Becoming Intellectually Virtuous.* Leicester: Apollos/Downers Grove: IVP, 1998.

Index of Names

Albert the Great, 75
Aldridge, David, 50
Al-Ghazali, 75
Alston, William, 4, 103, 119
Ambrose of Milan, 65
Ambrosiaster, 87
Anaxarchus, 19
Anscombe, G. E. M., 131
Anselm of Canterbury, 69
Apel, Karl-Otto, 80
Aquinas, Thomas, 9, 10, 11, 65, 70, 75–76, 86, 19, 123, 141
Aristides, 72
Aristotle, 4, 21, 68, 73, 75, 98, 102, 132, 141
Athenagoras of Athens, 72
Atkinson, James, 25, 37
Augustine of Hippo, 22, 65, 76, 70, 73–74, 75, 87
Austin, J. L. 131
Austin, Victor Lee, 34, 42–43
Averroes, 75
Avicenna, 75
Ayer, A. J., 111–12, 118

Balmer, Johann, 106
Barrett, C. K., 136
Barth, Gerhard, 64
Barth, Karl, 67, 68–69, 76, 87–89, 119, 125–26

Beale, Nicholas, 105
Belnap, N. D., 48
Beneke, Friedrich, 97
Berkeley, George, 54, 97
Beza, Theodore, 25
Bird, Michael, 8
Bohr, Niels, 106, 107
Bonhoeffer, Dietrich, 5
Born, Max, 107
Bornkamm, Günther, 70, 77, 88
Boullier, David, 25
Bourdin, Pierre, 29
Boyd, Gregory, 2
Briggs, C. A., 62
Briggs, Richard S., 42–44
Brown, Colin, 42
Brown, F., 62
Brown, Raymond, 137
Brunner, Emil, 68, 125–26
Bruns, Gerald, 49
Bultmann, Rudolf, 6, 7, 58, 64, 66, 67, 70, 81, 88, 136

Caird, George B., 58
Calvin, John, 11, 22, 24, 29, 77, 78–79, 88, 119, 123, 124
Carnap, Rudolf, 111
Cavell, Stanley, 57
Chadwick, Owen, 57

Index of Names

Index of Subjects

Index of Scripture